11·22·78

ADDING ROOMS, SAVING ENERGY
Upstairs, Downstairs, Sideways

ADDING ROOMS, SAVING ENERGY
Upstairs, Downstairs, Sideways

William M. Cowan

Macmillan Publishing Co., Inc.
NEW YORK

Collier Macmillan Publishers
LONDON

Macmillan Publishing Co., Inc.
866 Third Avenue, New York, N.Y. 10022
Collier Macmillan Canada, Ltd.

Library of Congress Cataloging in Publication Data

Cowan, William M
    Adding rooms, saving energy.

    Bibliography: p.
    Includes index.
    1. Dwellings—Remodeling. 2. Dwellings—
Energy Conservation. I. Title.
TH4816.C73 1979   643'.7   78-22033
ISBN 0-02-528540-8
ISBN 0-02-000280-7 pbk.

First Printing 1979

Printed in the United States of America

CONTENTS

1

TO MOVE
OR NOT

Almost everyone would like a house with more space—more "elbow room"—more places to "do things." We'd enjoy having areas that are less busy, confusing, and noisy. More living space—that's what so many families want and need.

Acquiring more space involves making one of three decisions: (1) buy a larger house, (2) add to the existing structure, or (3) find a way to gain more room within the present house space.

Building a large house is extremely expensive. So is buying a larger house that has already been built. Even adding a wing or dormer can be costly.

There are many reasons for the high costs. The price of land has skyrocketed almost everywhere. The cost of lumber and other building materials has doubled in the last few years. Mortgage interest rates are high, ranging from over eight percent to nine percent and more, depending on the area of the country, and the policies and ratings of the individual bank or loan company. Moving also involves broker's commissions, lawyers' fees, and expenses such as moving vans, disconnecting and reconnecting utilities, perhaps staying in a motel overnight or longer, and many other costs.

Another factor is the increasing cost of energy. Since 1974, the cost of electricity, oil, gas, and even wood have doubled—making essentials such as heating and air conditioning important cost considerations in building or buying a larger house.

What everyone's attic looks like until it's converted into bright and lively living space.

1

What was once a dark attic area became a bright bedroom and play area for the children. (Courtesy American Plywood Association)

A former garage opening becomes a conversation setting in this room designed by Barbara A. Egner. (Courtesy Waverly Fabrics)

Sewing corner, conversation couch, guest room - all in what
was once a dusty attic. (Courtesy Carefree Wallcoverings)

A new addition to the family deserves an additional room in the house. (Courtesy Imperial Wallcoverings)

TAKE A SECOND LOOK AT YOUR HOME

Unless you must move, the possibilities of adding more room within the space of your present home should be considered.

Look everywhere. The upstairs, downstairs, the attic, and basement may not be laid out and utilized as efficiently as they might be. This is especially true of older houses—particularly those built before World War II—which were designed and constructed before housing became standardized and when space and materials were more abundant and less costly.

Another possible area for expansion is an attached garage or carport that could be converted into a convenient and useful bedroom, study, or family room.

In this do-it-yourself book, you'll see how easily more room can be added while using space already available.

Adding a Bedroom

For many families, the most urgent need is another bedroom. Sometimes it is necessary for a growing youngster. Often it's needed because a parent, or an uncle, aunt, or other relative must be more conveniently located with the family.

Before designing and constructing an upstairs bedroom (or any other room or space), it's worthwhile to think about who will use the room. A son or daughter will have different needs and preferences than a parent, aunt, or uncle. A young

An unfinished attic became an imaginative, colorful bedroom for a child. (Photo by the makers of Armstrong Flooring, Carpets, and Ceiling Systems.)

Once there was a creepy, cobwebbed attic but someone made it into a light, spacious living room. (Courtesy Velux-America, Inc.)

person might not mind low, sloping ceilings as much as an adult. On the other hand, an adult might prefer being located slightly away from a busy and sometimes noisy family.

You'll also want to think ahead a few years. If a son or daughter plans to attend college away from home, what will be the primary use of the room then?

Adding a Guest Room

Many home areas are not used simply because they aren't "perfect"—neatly squared up with adequate ceiling heights.

Do they need to be perfect? Perhaps you have enough rooms for every purpose except a guest room, and you've dismissed the idea because the ceiling is low, with little headspace, and the rest of the area is limited by kneewalls.

Stop and think for a few minutes about the needs of your guests. How much time do they

spend in a room when they visit? Not very much. Just the hours they sleep there. Most of the time they're visiting with you in the living room, family room, or kitchen. Or they're outside your house altogether, sightseeing or visiting other friends.

An upstairs area that may be uncomfortable, small and even cramped for year-round living may be entirely suitable for sleeping purposes for a few days or even a week or two.

Adding a Recreation Room

Many a family has deprived itself of a fun-filled recreation or family room simply because the basement of the house is poorly laid out.

You know the type of basement arrangement: the furnace at one end, the sink, washing machine, and dryer at the other, and in between there's a stairway.

Consider some of the possibilities available. Can't one section of the basement accommodate a

Doors of these "closets" can be opened to create a private area
in which to study. (Courtesy of Handy Andy)

Once a carport, now a comfortable living area. Room design by Barbara A. Egner. (Courtesy Waverly Fabrics)

Before: With the proper tools and a little knowledge of construction a seldom used basement can be converted to an environment that makes relaxing more fun and studying tolerable for the reluctant student. (Courtesy of Handy Andy)

small recreation room? And the other section a study?

Don't give up easily. The purpose of this book is to help you find ways to obtain more room within your existing house space and do it economically.

Adding a Study

Many of us have dreamed of having a private study or library, book-lined and comfortable like those in mansions and private clubs. Here again, the attic, basement, or garage can be converted into a study or private library that is handsomely paneled, lined with books, and built-in stereo and television cabinets. True, it may never be as large, plush, antique filled, or chandeliered as those in the Vanderbilt or Roosevelt mansions, but why give up your dreams entirely?

Creating Privacy Areas

Most families complain of the lack of privacy. They need a place where a member of the family can get away from interruptions and read, sew, enjoy a hobby, or simply pay bills and balance the checkbook.

You should think about your family's special needs and interests. Even a relatively small area— 5' wide x 6' or 8' long with just enough headspace—can often be converted into useful, interesting, and valuable space.

Here are some examples:

A Sewing Nook or Corner. Where do you sew now? In the kitchen, bedroom, or family room?

That could mean picking up after each sewing session. A small corner or cranny, not much larger than your machine and table, can easily be built into a corner or nook that is as creative and beautiful as any you've seen in a home furnishings magazine. Decorated with different pieces of material, it could become one of the showplaces of your home.

A Hobby Corner. Does someone in the family collect stamps or butterflies, posters of baseball and football players, or travel posters and road maps or guides?

A drab area in the attic or basement can be turned into a room that is active and alive with interest.

A Reading Alcove. Sometimes it's nice to get away from everyone, curl up and finish reading a good

After: Beams and heating ducts can be concealed with a suspended ceiling and ceiling tiles. Paneling creates recessed areas for the television and bookshelves. (Courtesy of Handy Andy)

Ever dream of a quiet corner beside a roof window where there is light enough to sew? (Courtesy Velux-America, Inc.)

Attic space can become a stereo hi-fi leisure area. (Photo by the makers of Armstrong Flooring, Carpets, and Ceiling Systems.)

book. A reading alcove, lined with bookcases and shelves, and properly lighted, is the perfect place.

TV-Watching Area. Why argue about who'll watch what and where? A corner of the attic or basement can be set aside as a small television room. Decorate the room with photos of TV celebrities or favorite sports stars.

A Darkroom. Still send your photos out for processing or do you develop them in the bathroom? Why not build a darkroom in the basement, sectioning off a small area where you can work undisturbed?

The Home Office. Nothing is more annoying than trying to balance a checkbook in the middle of the living room or kitchen. Not a great deal of space is needed for a home office. An area large enough for a desk, a chair or two, and perhaps a filing cabinet will do nicely.

If you have a business sideline or your job requires you to take work home, you may be able to claim tax deductions. Specifically, you can deduct expenses related to your business income such as proportionate amounts of utility and main-tenance costs and other items. But a word of caution: the Internal Revenue Service insists that home offices be *bona fide* business areas. So check with the IRS or a tax specialist to be sure your home office qualifies.

MORE SPACE–MORE VALUE

There are many advantages to having more space in your house. It can mean more room for family activities, less confusion and noise, fewer instances of having to double up, and other benefits.

More space can also mean added value. Instead of a four-room house, you can now own a house with five, six, or even seven rooms as shown in Figs. 1–1 and 1–2. Instead of a four-room house, you can own a house with seven or more rooms as shown in Figs. 1–3 and 1–4. If you decide to sell your house at a later date, you could find that the additional living space also adds to the value of the house, and will give you a higher selling price.

While you're adding more space, you can also

Fig. 1-1 Anyone's four-room house (kitchen, living room and two bedrooms) before attic, basement, or carport are made into finished rooms. (Courtesy of Creative Services)

Fig. 1-2 Now it's a seven-room house with more privacy, comfort, living space. (Courtesy of Creative Services)

build in features that reduce operating costs. Insulating will save you money in the long run and can eventually repay part of the investment you make to add space.

Something else: home improvement costs are sometimes tax deductible when you sell a house, partially offsetting capital gains. So there's another reason for making more room in your home.

This do–it–yourself book provides many of the instructions for the work you'll need to do. It also contains many time–, money–, and energy–saving ideas. For some projects, such as installing electrical and plumbing fixtures, heating, air conditioning, and solar systems, you will need additional information. So read, ask questions, and learn.

Check with your local building inspectors. There are many building codes and regulations that vary from place to place. These inspectors can inform you about the regulations and can sometimes help you with practical advice.

Check with local suppliers—hardware, building supply, and home center dealers—and with local contractors. Many will give you helpful suggestions as to what is done locally. This is important because what is practical in one area of the USA may not be practical in another. And, of course, you alone are responsible for the workmanship and quality of your project.

Browse through building supply and hardware stores so that you become familiar with the tools and materials available. Ask friends, neighbors, and strangers. Don't be afraid to ask questions; no one knows everything.

Before you start your project, read this book from beginning to end. It will give you a basic idea of the work involved and the materials and tools needed. Decide what you would like to do before you begin. If you need to install heating or air-conditioning units in an upstairs room, this work will need to be performed before paneling or

Make your attic space into a handsome suite, complete with a
quiet corner for chess. (Courtesy Burlington Industries)

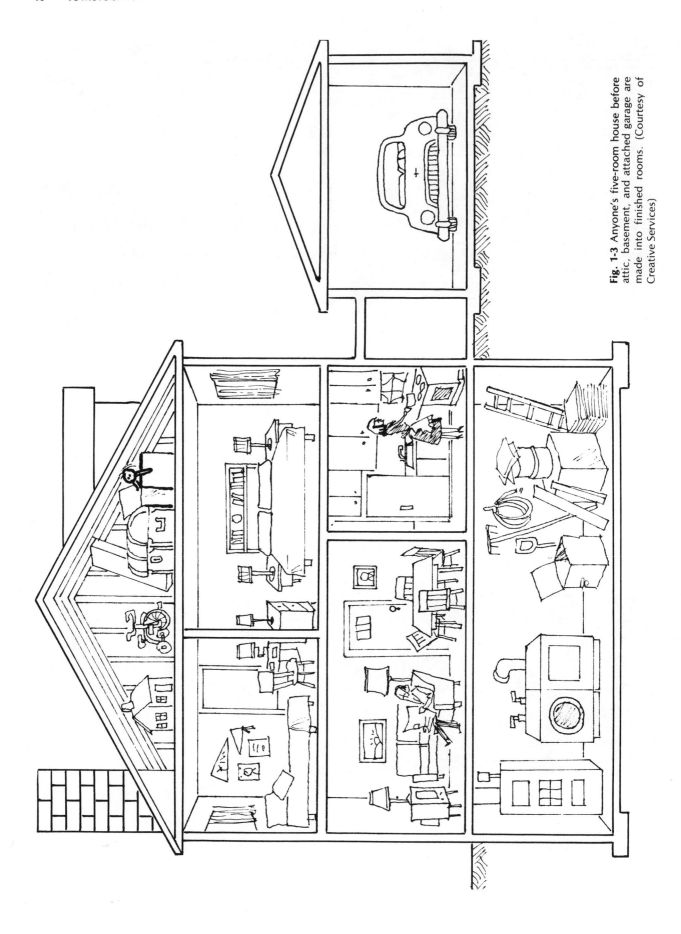

Fig. 1-3 Anyone's five-room house before attic, basement, and attached garage are made into finished rooms. (Courtesy of Creative Services)

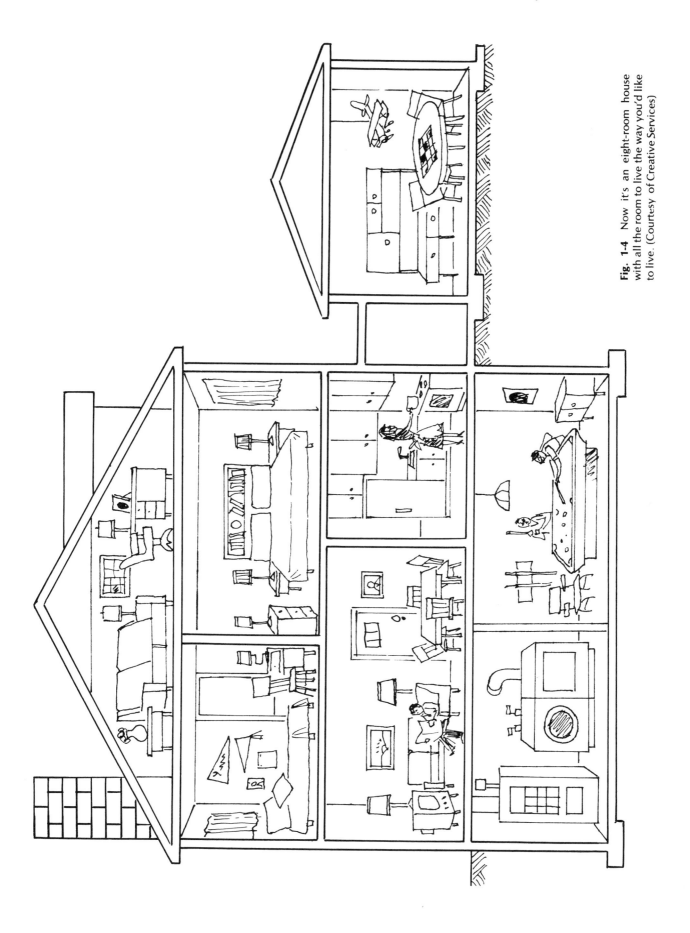

Fig. 1-4 Now it's an eight-room house with all the room to live the way you'd like to live. (Courtesy of Creative Services)

papering and other finishing tasks. Most likely additional wiring, plumbing, heating, and air conditioning will need to be installed by specialists who are licensed contractors. You'll also need to decide whether you want to install a solar hot-water heating system, roof windows, or an outside doorway to that basement recreation room before you start the finishing work.

That's why the next chapter is titled "Think before you tinker." Know what you want to do. Learn how to do it. Then go ahead and make more room for comfort and fun in your home.

2

THINK BEFORE YOU TINKER

Some people plow into a project before they know what they expect to accomplish.

You're obviously not that kind of person because you're reading this book. You *know* what you want to accomplish, whether it's adding a bedroom in the attic, making the basement into a rumpus room, or converting the garage into the nicest-looking recreation room on your street. You have an objective, and now you need to *make a plan*.

MAKE A COMPLETE PLAN

Making a complete plan will take a few hours now, but will save many hours later. Begin by taking detailed measurements of the area you intent to renovate. *Don't* guess your attic space is simply 8' high x 10' wide x 20' long and start buying materials, because if your house has high sloping rafters (and many houses do), your estimates will be completely wrong. You'll over-buy and then need to return materials to the home center or building supply yard, all of which takes time and costs money.

Instead, first make a rough sketch of the area noting the principal dimensions. Use a sheet of graph paper, letting each square equal one foot or one yard (Fig. 2-1). Keep in mind that wallboard and paneling usually come in 4' wide x 8' long sections. Figure the necessary allowances for doors and windows, and get a rough idea of the shapes of sections that will need to be cut from wallboards and panels.

Be sure to include lighting, plumbing, heating, and air-conditioning fixtures in your plan if you intend to install new ones. In many cases, installing these fixtures, along with their in-wall wiring and plumbing, is the first step in the project. So make rough diagrams of the circuits and pipelines, too.

Before you begin work is the time to make decisions. Nothing is more aggravating than having to redo a project because of poor planning. Visualize how you'll furnish the area, whether to place a bed or a billiard table in the room, or to set aside a corner for a sewing machine or television set.

To help you plan in detail, there is a 3-D PLAN-IT-KIT that enables you to visualize furniture, paint and wallpaper, drapes and curtains, and pictures and paintings as they would appear in your home. One of these kits gives you 150 combinations, and enables you to arrange three rooms at the same time. It costs $9.50 and can also be used to visualize other room layouts and decorations. (The 3-D PLAN-IT-KIT is available from PLAN-IT-KIT, Inc., Box 429, Westport, Conn. 06880.)

TOOLS FOR THE TASK

The tools you will need are conventional, few in number, and relatively inexpensive. You probably already own most of them: hammer, saw, screwdrivers, etc.

A radial arm saw or drill press with all the latest features and attachments is great, but owning one isn't always necessary. A friend or neighbor might let you use his equipment; or have the work done at a lumberyard where millwork costs are substantially less than the price of a brand-new radial saw. Renting tools is another possibility.

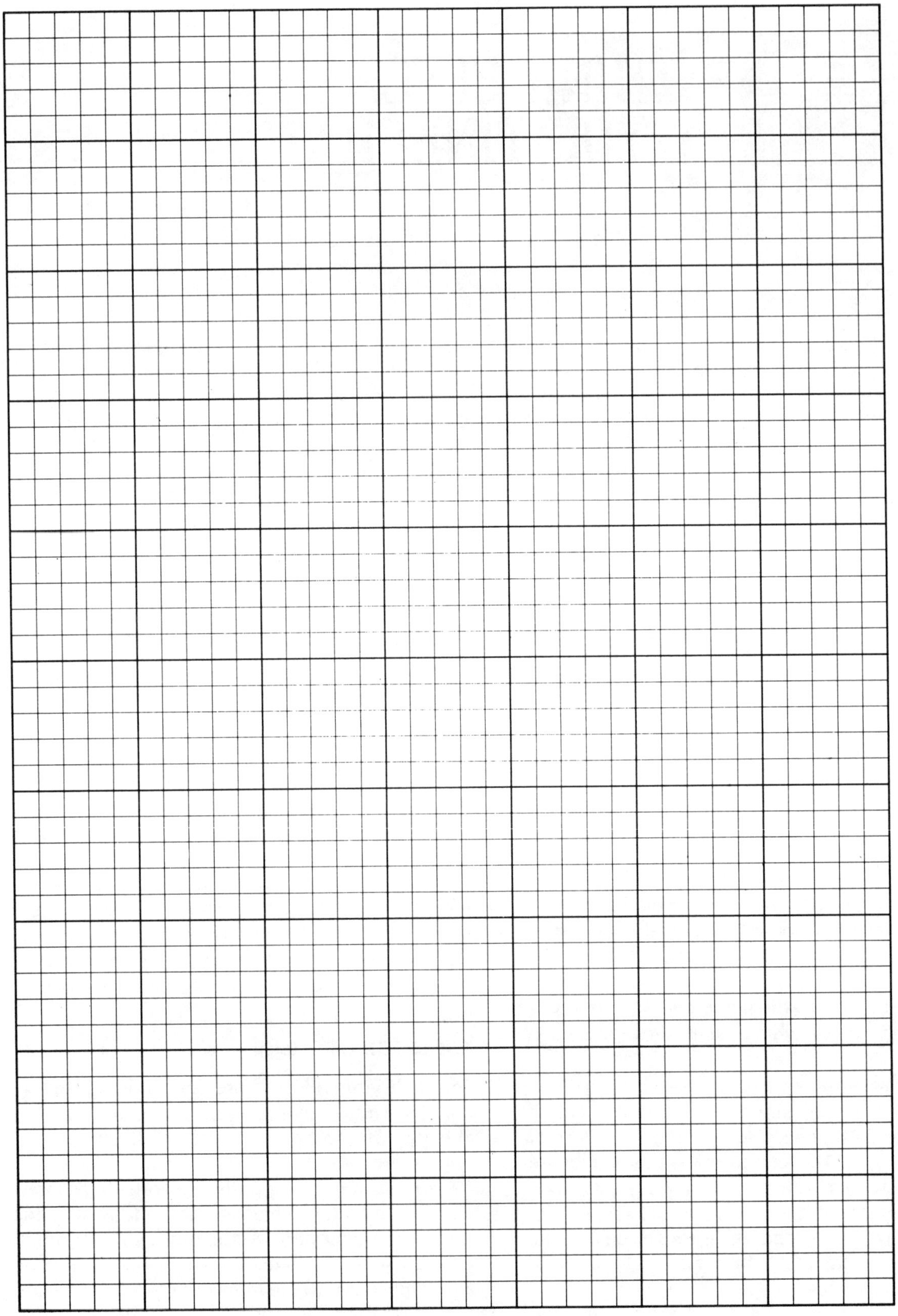

Fig. 2-1   Make a plan, figuring each square = 1 sq. ft.

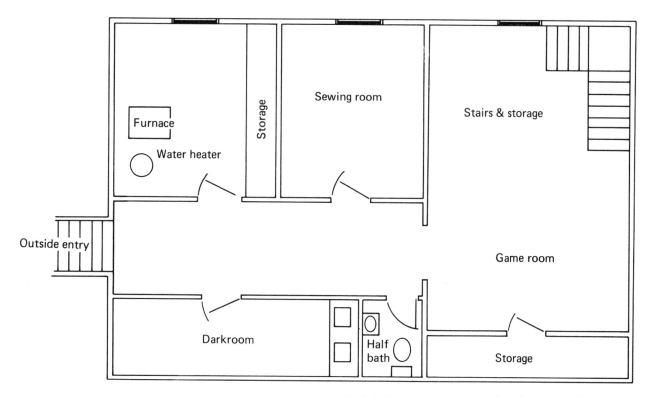

Fig. 2-1 Before starting work make a floor plan of how you'll divide basement into liveable areas. (Courtesy *The Home Repair Book*, J. G. Ferguson Publishing Co.)

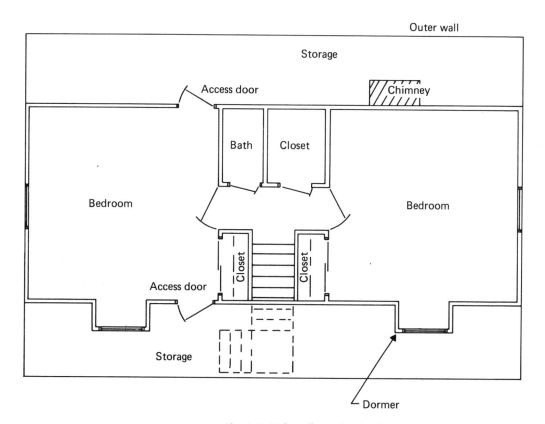

Fig. 2-2 Make a floor plan for the new bedrooms before you start work. Doing so can make the task more efficient, minimize changes. (Courtesy *The Home Repair Book*, J. G. Ferguson Publishing Co.)

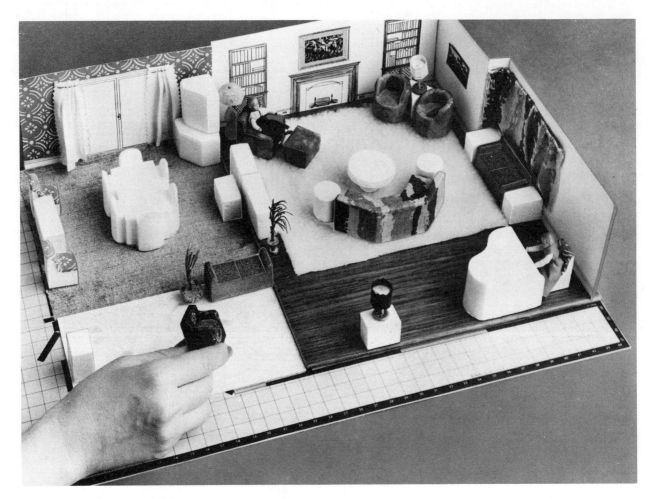

PLAN-IT-KIT enables you to visualize room arrangements and furnishings. (Photo courtesy PLAN-IT-KIT, Inc.)

Here's a checklist of the basic tools you'll need. Check those you don't own and plan to purchase them when they are on sale (or find out from whom you can borrow them).

For Woodworking/Insulating, etc.

Hammer – claw type. Handle and heft several sizes until you find one that feels comfortable to you.

Saw [hand]. Cross-cut, with 8 to 10 teeth per inch.

Saw [keyhole]. With an assortment of blade sizes.

Screwdrivers. Small, medium, and large blades and Phillips. A selection always comes in handy.

Tape/flexible rule. A 16' length is convenient to use.

Utility Knife. With retractable blade for safety.

Chisel[s]. At least two types: one 6" long with a 1" blade, the other a butt chisel 3" long with 1" blade.

Mallet. To use with chisels although most of us will use a hammer and even a rock!

File[s]. Single- and double–cut, and a wood rasp. Here again, an assortment is always useful.

Plane[s]. A small block plane is convenient, but better work requires a larger, two–handed smoothing or jack plane.

Square. A 2' long square is worth the investment but you may be able to get by with a smaller one.

Level[s]. Two sizes are helpful: a short 6" torpedo type level and a 2' long carpenter's level.

Stapler. Compression type, capable of handling ½" wide staples.

An in-home office can be as elegant looking as you like once you've renovated the attic area. (Courtesy Burlington Industries)

An ugly attic can become an imaginative combination living area and playroom. (Photo by the makers of Armstrong Flooring, Carpets and Ceiling Systems)

Miter Box and Saw. For straight and angle cuts in wood, conduit, tubing.

Studfinder. To locate uprights behind wallboard, paneled or plastered walls.

Stepladder. Unless you are a professional basketball player, you'll need one.

Chalk string. To snap chalklines.

Plumbline. For lining things up vertically. Use a string and a weight (but make sure the weight falls straight—*don't* use a hammer or other tool likely to pull the string to one side).

Power Tools

Sander. Double–insulated, straight–line finishing type.

Saber or Jig Saw. Double–insulated, with a selection of blades.

Rotary or Circular Saw. Double–insulated with a 7″ blade. A saber is used more often than a rotary. If you need both, invest in a saber and borrow a rotary.

Drill. Electric drills always come in handy. Buy a sturdy ½″ double–insulated one and an assortment of bits.

Ideas turned one attic into the swinging-est room in the neighborhood. (Photo by the makers of Armstrong Flooring, Carpets and Ceiling Systems)

For Electrical Work

Pliers. Long–nose types are essential.

Pliers–diagonal cutting. For cutting and splicing wires, although wire-strippers are useful, too.

Hacksaw and blades. To cut BX, tubing, and conduit. A rugged one will also cut through pipe.

Fishtape. This is a long piece of wire with "fish-hooks" at both ends, and is essential if you extend wiring from floor to floor.

Crimper. A plier–like tool for crimping wires into connectors. You can use pliers if you are dextrous.

Soldering iron. For electrical and plumbing tasks.

For Plumbing Work

Pipe wrench. A 10" Stilson; it will also come in handy for loosening and tightening bolts on you car.

Propane gas torch. For joining pipes, fittings, etc., and also removing layers and layers of paint.

Hacksaw. A rugged hacksaw will also cut through BX and conduit. (See tools for electrical work above.)

Tubing cutter. Borrow one unless your project is extensive or you plan to become a plumber.

For Painting/Papering

Brushes, rollers, pad, or sponge applicators

Scrapers	*Caulking gun*	
Putty knife	*Razor knife*	
Drop cloths	*Pasting brush*	
Scissors	*Smoothing brush*	
Straight edge	*Seam roller*	
Sponge[s]	*Plumb or chalk line*	

Insulating Materials

___ *Batts, rolls, panels*

___ *Caulking compound*

___ *Weatherstripping*

___ *Staples*

___ *Wire [or chickenwire]*

___ *Loose fill insulation*

These are the basic tools. You probably own many of them, and need to buy others. You may also want to consider borrowing or renting more expensive tools that will only be used once. How much you spend for them depends on the likelihood of future usage. A good hammer, for example, can last a lifetime. On the other hand, unless you expect to use a power drill, saw, or sander for many more projects, the moderately priced, do-it–yourself models should be sufficient. The price difference between amateur and professional models can range as high as forty or fifty dollars. Unless you happen to purchase a lemon that fails immediately after warranty, the moderately priced model should be adequate.

...AND THE MATERIALS

A detailed list of the materials needed for *every* attic/basement/garage renovation could be very extensive. However, the following checklist will help you avoid running short of materials just when you need them. It may also help you make firm decisions such as whether to paint or panel. (More than one experienced do–it–yourselfer has changed courses in midstream!)

Another reason for the checklist is that it can help you plan your purchasing. Knowing what you need will enable you to take advantage of seasonal sales. You can also purchase when items are on sale at different stores. We've all had the experience of buying lumber, paint, tools, or whatever at one store and finding the same items selling at a lower price elsewhere.

How much you can save by planned purchasing is difficult to estimate. But savings could amount to as much as five or ten percent of the total project cost, which is money easily used to pay bills or make other purchases.

Lumber/Wood/Finishing Materials

___ *2 x 4's and other wood as planned.*

___ *Molding[s]*

___ *Plywood*

___ *Sheathing*

___ *Panels*

___ *Adhesives*

___ *Sandpaper*

___ *Nails [assortment]*

___ *Wallboard*

___ *Tape*

___ *Screws [assortment]*

___ *Tile [wall/floor]*

___ *Carpeting*

___ *Windows [preframed]*

___ *Doors [preframed]*

___ *Solar panels*

___ *Skylight[s]*

___ *Attic fan[s]*

Electrical Materials

___ *Switches*

___ *Wiring*

___ *BX/sheathed cable*

___ *Wiring*

___ *Conduit*

___ *Connectors*

Refer to this chart for correct nail lengths. Proper nail use minimizes splintering, provides better holding power. (Courtesy *The Home Repair Book*, J. G. Ferguson Publishing Co.)

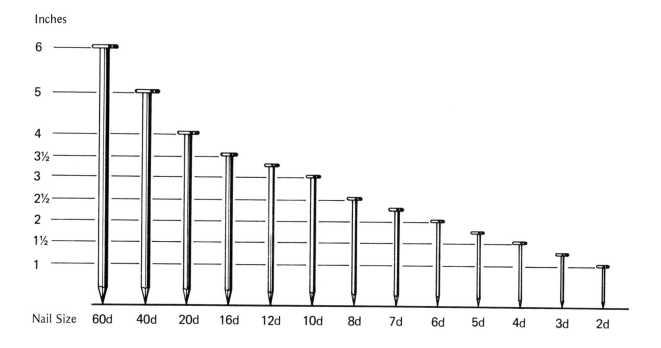

Inches

| 6 |
| 5 |
| 4 |
| 3½ |
| 3 |
| 2½ |
| 2 |
| 1½ |
| 1 |

Nail Size   60d   40d   20d   16d   12d   10d   8d   7d   6d   5d   4d   3d   2d

____ *Electrical tape*

____ *Electrical boxes*

____ *Outlets* [*receptacles*]

____ *Solder*

____ *Fixtures*

____ *Switch Plates*

Plumbing Materials

____ *Fixtures* [*sink, shower, tub, toilet*]

____ *Pipe*

____ *Tubing*

____ *Elbows*

____ *Pipe unions*

____ *T–joints*

____ *Insulation* [*pipe*]

____ *Compound*[*s*]

____ *Flux*

Paint/Wallpaper

____ *Paint*[*s*]

____ *Wallpaper*[*s*]

____ *Thinner*

____ *Paint remover*

____ *Paste*

____ *Razor blades*

____ *Spackle*

____ *Sandpaper*

____ *Masking tape*

Table 2–1 Nail Sizes and Weights.

Penny (d) Size	Length(in.)	Common	Finishing
2	1	850	—
3	1 1/4	545	875
4	1 1/2	295	600
6	2	170	300
8	2 1/2	100	200
10	3	65	-
12	3 1/4	60	-
16	3 1/2	45	-
20	4	30	-
30	4 1/2	20	-

*The number of nails per pound varies somewhat with the manufacturer.
(Courtesy *The Home Repair Book*, J.G. Ferguson Publishing Co.)

WHEN TO START

The best time to start your project may depend on the geographical area and the climate where you live. In many areas, spring and fall are the best seasons for remodeling activities. The weather then is best suited for insulating an attic, beginning construction of an outside door to the basement playroom, or closing in a carport or garage.

Long holiday weekends and vacations make good starting times because you can complete a major part of your project and see it taking shape. Working steadily, you can complete more of the major tasks (wiring, plumbing, insulating, paneling, painting or wallpapering), leaving the "fill–in" jobs for evenings or a convenient weekend.

3

"ROUGHING IN"
THE ATTIC

The starting point for roughing in your attic will depend on its present condition. Is it an open area without *any* flooring, partially or completely rough–floored, or does it have a finished floor?

Let's take the worst situation first, no floor at all. You will certainly need one on which to stand, squat, kneel, and rest. But should you finish flooring the attic if you are planning to add electrical wiring, plumbing and insulation?

Start with a half measure, and give yourself a place to stand. You could rough–floor only an area that would not interfere with later work; but put safety first. Lay down all the floor panels knowing you'll need to remove one or two later.

First, a few words about subflooring. Most floor joists, the long beams under the flooring (or exposed if there is no flooring), are spaced 16" o.c. (on center). This means that the distance from the center of one joist to the center of the next measures 16".

As most panels measure 4' wide x 8' long, you will be able to lay the 4' width of one panel across four joists, leaving 1" of space on each outside joist to accomodate the next panel. If a panel edge or end does not rest on a joist, you will need to support it with blocking using a 2 x 4 nailed between the joists and leveled with their tops as shown in Fig. 3-1. Use 8d (2½"-long) nails, spacing them 6" to 10" apart to fasten the panels.

Stagger the panels so that their edges and ends center as much as possible on different floor joists. Leave 1/8" space between the panel edges and 1/16" between the ends. The technical drawing in Fig. 3-1 shows typical flooring construction.

Plywood panels or sheets is the usual subflooring material. You could use ½"-thick panels, but

they might become "bouncy." Instead, 5/8" to 3/4" thicknesses are recommended.

Plywood subflooring or underlayment can also be glued and nailed, using a special technique and estastomeric adhesives, which will increase floor stiffness and minimize squeaking. However, do *not* use this method unless the floor is to be permanent—so you *won't* need to raise some of the panels for electrical or plumbing connections.

Now that you have a floor on which to stand, you can begin working on the partition(s) you planned.

PARTITIONING THE ATTIC

Attic areas less than four feet in height are ususally partitioned off as storage or waste space. But if your roof does not slope too steeply, you may be able to use part of this area for built–in cabinets or storage space.

Fig. 3-2 show the typical framing for an attic wall partition and the ceiling. The wall partitions are referred to as "kneewalls." Notice how the uprights or studs rest on a "floor plate" and also how the uprights are strengthened by horizontal crosspieces or "blocking."

To start a partition, measure the distances and height (usually 4' high or more) you select at one end of the attic. Drop a plumbline (a length of string with a weight on one end to make the line fall straight), and mark rafter and floor. Repeat this procedure at the opposite end of the area you plan to partition.

Now snap a chalkline between these two points. To make a chalkline, stretch a string between the points you've marked, fastening it

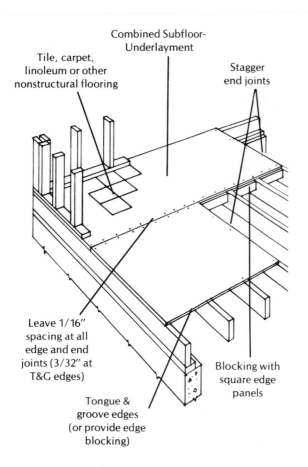

Tile, carpet, linoleum or other nonstructural flooring

Combined Subfloor-Underlayment

Stagger end joints

Leave 1/16" spacing at all edge and end joints (3/32" at T&G edges)

Tongue & groove edges (or provide edge blocking)

Blocking with square edge panels

Fig. 3-1 Combined subfloor–underlayment. Note that floor panels are supported by joists and blocking. (Courtesy American Plywood Association)

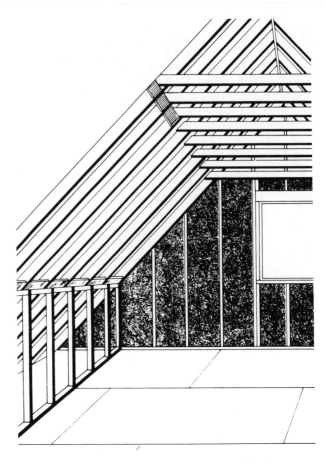

Fig. 3-2 Typical attic partitioning. Space at left of partition (kneewall) is waste or storage space. (Courtesy *The Home Repair Book,* J. G. Ferguson Publishing Co.)

with thumbtacks or nails at both ends. Chalk the string. Now snap it, quickly but carefully. Doing so will give you a straight chalkline between the two points. If you find using plumblines and chalklines difficult, you can measure the distances using a tape measure, yardstick, or even a board. The important thing is to make sure the lines are straight *and* perpendicular.

Now you can nail a floor plate or "shoe"—a 2 x 4—the length of the line. Use 16d (3½"-long) common nails with flat heads that will go through the 2" thickness of a 2 x 4 and the subflooring, and tighten securely into the joists.

If the partition line runs perpendicular to the rafters, you can cut studs to length and nail them between the shoe and rafters, spacing them 16" apart center to center. Studs can be nailed to the sides of the rafters, to a "top plate," or mitered (cut at an angle) to fit snugly under the rafters.

Support the studs by nailing 2 x 4 horizontal crosspieces, "blocks," or "cats" between them.

You may also need these crosspieces to support wallboard or paneling.

If you divide the attic area so that you cannot nail studs directly to the rafters or a top plate, you may need to "raise" a partition like the one shown in Fig. 3–3.

Cut 2 x 4 plates, one for the bottom or "shoe" and the other for the top of the partition. These must be the length of the partition planned. Lay them side by side. Mark the positions for the studs, 16" on center, across both shoes and allow space for the door, which is usually 30" or 38" wide. (Preassembled door frames are readily available today and more convenient than erecting a frame yourself. Check the frame size before allowing space for the door on the bottom plate.) Use a square to make sure that the lines are straight and perpendicular.

Ideally, you will have enough room to assemble the partition and then raise it. Brace the plates so they won't slip, then nail through the plates into

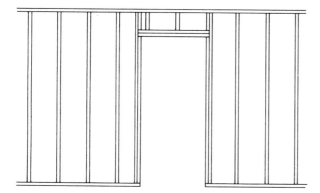

Fig. 3-3 Framework for a partition separating the attic into two rooms. (Courtesy *The Home Repair Book,* J. G. Ferguson Publishing Co.)

the studs. Raise the partition. Check again, to make sure plates and studs are square, and then nail into rafters and joists.

If you should decide to make your own door frame, you will need to cut 2 x 4's to length and nail them to the supporting studs. Cap with 2 x 4 headers and add supporting 2 x 4 studs over the door frames and centered above the door. Last, cut the bottom plate or shoe to allow space for the door.

When attic space does not permit raising a partition, you can still construct one by installing top and bottom plates and "toenailing" into the studs. This is not as easy as raising a partition because more checking and rechecking needs to be done to make sure the plates run true and the studs stand straight and square.

Toenailing simply means nailing an upright or vertical stud to a floor plate or a horizontal piece of lumber. Drive the nail diagonally through the upright into the horizontal plate while bracing your shoe against the opposite side of the upright so that the upright doesn't move or slip while you drive the nail. Nail through the center of the upright and the plate so that the nail doesn't split the edges of the wood.

This general description of framing applies whether you "wall off" waste or storage space, or split a long attic area into two separate rooms. If you should decide to install cabinets or storage space behind the attic wall, you will need to partition off small triangular areas. Use 2 x 2's or a combination of 2 x 2 and 2 x 4 studs and plates in these smaller areas.

INSTALLING ROOF WINDOWS

Many attics have no windows or windows only at opposite ends. As shown in photos in this book,

roof windows can be very attractive and pleasing interior features. So, by planning ahead, you may decide to install one or more roof windows before you begin to put the finishing touches on your upstairs room or rooms.

Doing so offers a number of advantages. It provides natural lighting, thereby minimizing use of electricity. It also provides more light than is available with conventional dormers at considerably less expense. It may also provide a scenic view. Last, but not least, it should allow you to vent hot attic rooms during warm weather and may eliminate the need for an upstairs air conditioner.

Preassembled roof windows are available in a wide range of overall sizes. Standard sizes are available from 16" x 24" to 48" x 48" with special shapes and sizes ranging from 21 5/8" x 27 1/2" to 36 7/8" x 62 7/8" and 52 3/4" x 55 1/2". They are also available with two or three panes of glass and with shades to maximize cooling and minimize heat loss. When purchasing a roof window unit make sure that the contour of the bottom of the unit provides for drainage and prevents water from collecting.

In general, the higher you install the window the more light will be provided. On the other hand, installing the window a little lower may provide a scenic view. You will need to consider the location and installation carefully if you have small, climbing children.

You will also need to consider the exposure, although this will be dictated by the direction your house faces. A roof window facing south or southeast will provide morning light, and one facing north and west will provide late afternoon and early evening light.

There are several manufacturers of preassembled roof window units. Directions are included with the kits. (If not, telephone the dealer and demand them!) But here is a brief description of what's involved:

1. Determine the location and measure an area the size of the roof window unit's outside edge (the "curb") on the inside of the roof. Allow an additional 1" or so all around for easier placement of the unit in the hole.

2. Brace the rafter(s) to be cut by nailing 2 x 4's from the rafters to short floor plates. The braces should be located above and below the hole area.

3. Erect a scaffold or build a platform on the outside of the house, as most of your work will be done on the outside roof.

Installing flashing above a roof window. (Courtesy Velux-America, Inc.)

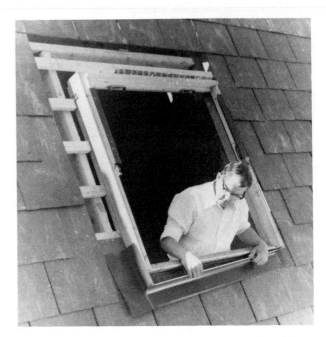

Installing flashing below the casing of a roof window. (Courtesy Velux-America, Inc.)

4. Saw the rafter(s) at the predetermined length(s). Then saw through the sheathing and roofing.

5. Remove all shingle or roofing nails within 4–5 inches of the opening.

6. Set the roof window in place, fastening it to the roof with the fasteners provided or using L-shaped brackets. Use at least two brackets on each side, locating them near the corners.

7. Cut four strips of aluminum or copper flashing, measured to fold over the edge of the window roof curb and to extend 4–5 inches beyond the roof opening.

8. Bend the flashing into position and nail to the edges of the curb as shown in photographs 3–1 and 3–2.

9. Lift shingles and nail flashing through the sheathing. If flashing overlaps, make sure the overlap faces downward in order to drain rain water and melting snow.

10. Solder the abutting corners of the flashing or bond then with a flashing epoxy.

11. Reshingle around the roof window unit as needed but do not nail through the flashing. Apply a cement or waterproofing compound over the nailheads to eliminate seepage.

12. Bond around the roof window unit frame or curb with a thick but neat layer or ribbon of waterproofing sealant.

13. Install optional fixtures. Some manufacturers offer devices for shading, tilting, or lowering windows, electric open–and–close, and insect screening. Directions for installing these fixtures should be provided with the fixtures.

While working on the outside roof, it's a good idea to check the condition of your roof, and replace loose or damaged shingles and flashing as necessary.

One last word, roof windows can enhance the appearance of the exterior and the interior of a home. But don't go overboard and overdo them. Consider the spacing carefully. You cannot cut every rafter without seriously affecting the roof and, in fact, your entire house! If you intend to place more than one or two roof windows on each side, consult an architect or a professional builder.

SOLAR HOT WATER SYSTEM

While planning to renovate, you might consider installing energy–saving devices such as a solar hot water heating system. Heating water for washing, shaving, bathing, dishwashing, washing clothes, and cleaning, accounts for a fairly substantial use of electricity, oil, or gas in the average home.

Fig. 3–4 shows a roof–mounted system consisting of solar panels (absorbers), storage tank, and

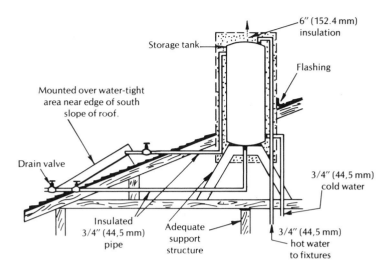

Fig. 3-4 Solar hot water heating system once widely used in Florida is regaining popularity. (Courtesy *Solar Energy: A Biased Guide*)

piping. Systems such as this one were once very popular in Florida, and are regaining popularity as a means of reducing energy costs. How well it will work for you depends on the number of days of sunshine in your area, general climate, and present and future hot–water heating costs. In New England, for example, materials and labor costs could run more than $1,000, while reducing energy expenses by only $30–40 a year. Thus, payback could take as long as 25–30 years. But if energy costs continues to double and triple every five years, payback would be realized much earlier.

The system shown here works similarly to coil-heated hot water systems. Water is circulated through tubing in the heated areas (absorbers) and then stored in a tank for future use.

A glass–cover absorber (also called a "collector" or "panel"), approximately 12′ x 4′, is needed with a tank size of 82 gallons. Maximum insulation is needed around the tank and tubing to prevent loss of heat as outside temperatures lower.

To install the system you will need to erect a sturdy platform to support the tank. An 82-gallon tank, insulated and filled with water, will weigh about 700 pounds, so you will need to set it on a solid structure supported by crossbraced 2 x 4's.

You will need to cut a hole through the roof slightly larger than the circumference of the tank, and also cut two holes to accomodate the 3/4″ piping to the absorbers. The absorbers are installed without cutting into the roof, but should be firmly supported by the uprights and fastened into the rafters.

Note that the cold–water piping enters and exits at the bottom of the tank while the hot–water piping enters and exits at the top of the tank. Note, too, that drain valves are located on the absorber-to-tank piping in order to drain the system, which should be done once or twice a year to minimize rust and corrosion.

The cold–water piping, of course, is connected to the incoming water supply line and the hot-water piping to sink, shower, and bathtub fixtures. So, unless your house is in the process of construction, it will be necessary to rip out existing piping.

Ground–mounted and awning–type solar collectors or systems are also available and may be better suited to your needs. A word of caution about solar–energy systems in general. Many, like the one shown above work best in high sunshine areas such as Miami, and are less effective elsewhere. A good discussion of solar–heating systems of different types is presented in *Solar Energy: A Biased Guide* by William I. Ewers. Read the book, collect more information, and talk to contractors before undertaking a solar–heating project.

ATTIC FANS

While your project is still in the rough stages, you might consider the advantages of installing an attic fan as a hot weather energy-saving device. North of New York City, for example, there are usually only ten or fifteen days a year when the weather makes you wish for air conditioning.

Installing an attic fan to exhaust hot air or bring in cool air may be entirely satisfactory for your purposes.

There are two general types: exterior wall-mounted fans and interior circulating fans. The exterior types exhaust hot air from the attic. (Reversible types will also bring cool air into the attic.) By moving the heavy hot-air blanket, they permit cool ground air to move up through the house. The procedure for mounting these fans is similar to that of installing a roof window except that you'll need to cut through the side of the house rather than the roof.

After selecting the location and taking your measurements, cut through the wall from the inside of the house, biting into the sheathing and then the outside shingles or clapboard.

Incidentally, it is a good idea when making initial cuts to saw an inch or two inside the perimeter rather than directly on the perimeter line. If the saw slips or you make a mistake, you can still cut out to the perimeter.

Exhaust fans are available as preassembled units with frames or casings in many sizes. If you select one less than 15" wide there should be no need to cut into the uprights. Larger sizes will require cutting into uprights and bracing following similar steps to those for installing a window (see the section on installing windows in carports and garages later in this book).

The second type of fan, interior circulating, was common in the days before air conditioning. Suspended from the ceiling, it moves the hot air, circulating it and pushing it away from the center of the room to the edges. This installation is similar to that for an overhead electrical fixture and should be made before finishing the ceiling.

Both types of fans, exterior and interior, are usually motor driven and often require the installation of a separate wiring circuit for their operation (see section on electricity/wiring for further information). Attic fans are not as effective as air conditioners, but may prove entirely suitable for your needs and be effective energy savers.

HEATING/AIR CONDITIONING

Installing anything more than a portable heating unit or air conditioner in an attic area deserves special consideration. Check carefully with experts before you plunge into the project.

The reasons for caution are (1) there are many variations in heating systems even though they use oil, gas, or electricity, and (2) heating systems are, or should be, properly sized to the requirements of the house.

When the heating system for your house was installed, it was probably sized to meet only the heating requirements of the finished rooms. It may or may not have been sized for future heating of an unfinished attic. It is very unlikely to have been sized to accommodate an unfinished basement and certainly not an attached carport or garage.

But don't let the fact that you *may* need a larger heating system discourage you. You may *not* need it. If you thoroughly insulate the room or area, additional heating (or air conditioning) may not be required. A great deal depends upon your geographic area and the uses of the room. Installing heating for just a few cold days, or air conditioning for a few hot days, may not justify the cost.

(Note: The same applies to a new downstairs or basement room. If you have insulated the heating pipes or ducts, remove the insulation to let warmth from the pipes help heat the room. However, it will probably be necessary to install heating units in a former garage or carport if portable units aren't sufficient for the task.)

The best advice is to check with a heating and air conditioning contractor, because you can't just cut into a pipe or two, install a union, and run piping to a new baseboard heating unit or radiator. If you do, you could throw the entire furnace or cooling system out of kilter, a fact you may not discover until next winter or summer. This could mean undoing and redoing all your finishing work.

Here's what is involved in determining the degree of heating needed in sizing a home heating system. First, the U factor must be calculated. This is the rate of heat flow in Btu/hr through one square foot of surface with a temperature of one degree Fahrenheit between the air on one side and the air on the other. U factors are calculated for walls, windows, and doors exposed to the outside. Factors for floors and ceilings must also be included. These factors are then mulitplied by local design temperatures which vary from Los Angeles, California, to Portland, Maine. Calculations should also be made for the heat loss around doors, windows, and cracks. Wind velocities are also factored into the calculations.

Central air conditioning systems are also sized. Considerations in estimating the K factors or Btu requirements for air conditioning include determining the total square footage of the floor area, type of ceiling and wall construction (including insulation), percentage of glass in the outside walls (and also whether the glass is single-, double- or triple-pane), ceiling height, temperatures, and location in relation to the sun.

In general, a one-ton air conditioning system will cool five to seven thousand cubic feet of residential space. If you must add air conditioning, consider supplementing the central system with smaller units that offer the advantages of energy savings when they are not needed.

Again, though, much depends on the use of the room. Remember: your grandparents or great-grandparents managed to live quite well without central heating *or* central air conditioning!

PLUMBING INSTALLATIONS

Think before you decide to install a bathroom in what was the attic and is now becoming an up-stairs room(s). If your present plumbing system suffers from inadequate water pressure, an upstairs bathroom won't help matters. Or, if your family complains about inadequate hot water, then a bathroom for new members of the family won't help either. Your basic hot-water system may need to be overhauled and a tank larger than your present one installed.

Also, if you live in a town or city with a community water supply you may not be allowed to make any new installation unless you engage a licensed plumber. The reason is simply that if you should connect the drainage system to the water-supply system you could endanger your family's health and that of others.

A brief description of plumbing systems, and what is involved in adding fixtures, will give you a better idea of the systems.

Basic Systems

There are two basic plumbing systems in a house: the water-supply system and the drainage (sometimes called the "waste" or "soil") system. Examples of the two systems are shown in Figures 3.5 and 3.6.

The supply system brings water into the house either from town or city water lines, or private wells. At the water heater, the supply system is usually divided into two lines: hot and cold. (Some lines, such as cold-water lines to outside faucets, may branch before reaching the heater.) Both

cold- and hot-water lines usually run parallel to the house and are concealed between ceilings and floors.

The vertical pipes extending between floors are called "risers" and are concealed in the walls. Most fixtures (sinks, bathtubs, toilets) have shutoff valves located just below the fixture (e.g., under the sink) but may be installed elsewhere, such as below the fixture but in the basement.

You can usually shut off the water supply to a fixture, but not always to a branch line. Therefore, you will usually need to shut off the entire system and drain it before installing new fixtures.

Drainage Systems   2038875

Water coming into the house must also go out. The drainage system carries waste and used water to the main house drain which is connected to a municipal sewage system or a septic tank.

In addition, each fixture connects to one of two vents. Toilets connect to the main vent and other fixtures to a secondary vent. These are the pipes you see sticking up through the roof of your house. The purpose of these vents is to seal off sewer gases and also to allow the plumbing systems to operate at outside air pressure. In very cold climates, these vents must be insulated.

Draining the System

You should know how to drain your water-supply and waste systems in case of an emergency, or in case local regulations permit you to make installations. The sequence is as follows:
1. Shut off electricity and/or gas used for home and water heating.
2. Close main shutoff valve which should be located outside the house.
3. Starting with upstairs facilities, open all faucets and flush all toilets.
4. Open and drain valves for water heater, furnace, water softener, etc.

The sequence changes in order to restore the water supply:
1. Close all drain valves (water heater, furnace, water softener, etc.)
2. Slowly open the main shutoff valve.
3. Turn off all faucets.
4. Turn on electricity and gas.

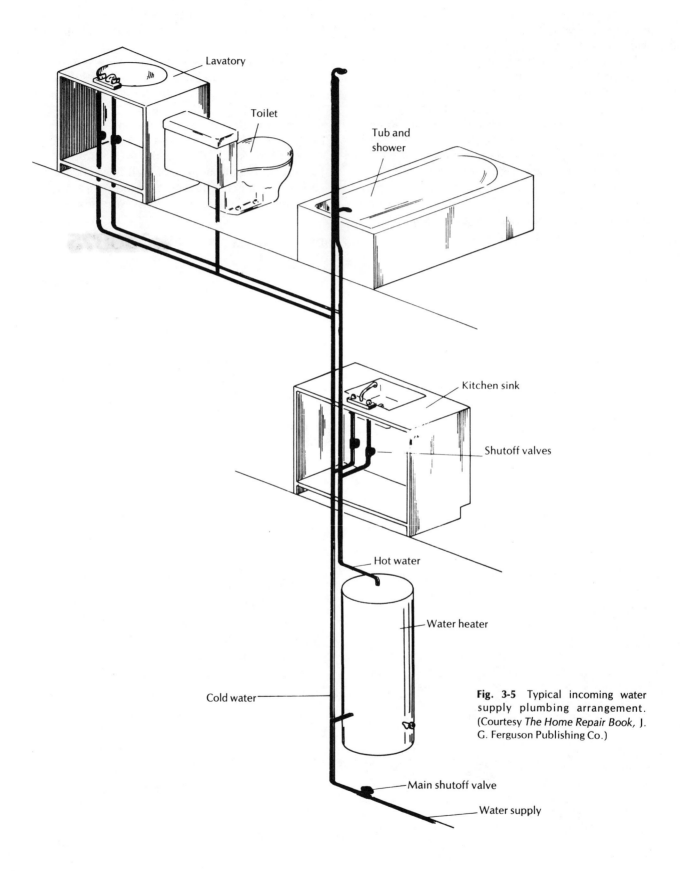

Fig. 3-5 Typical incoming water supply plumbing arrangement. (Courtesy *The Home Repair Book,* J. G. Ferguson Publishing Co.)

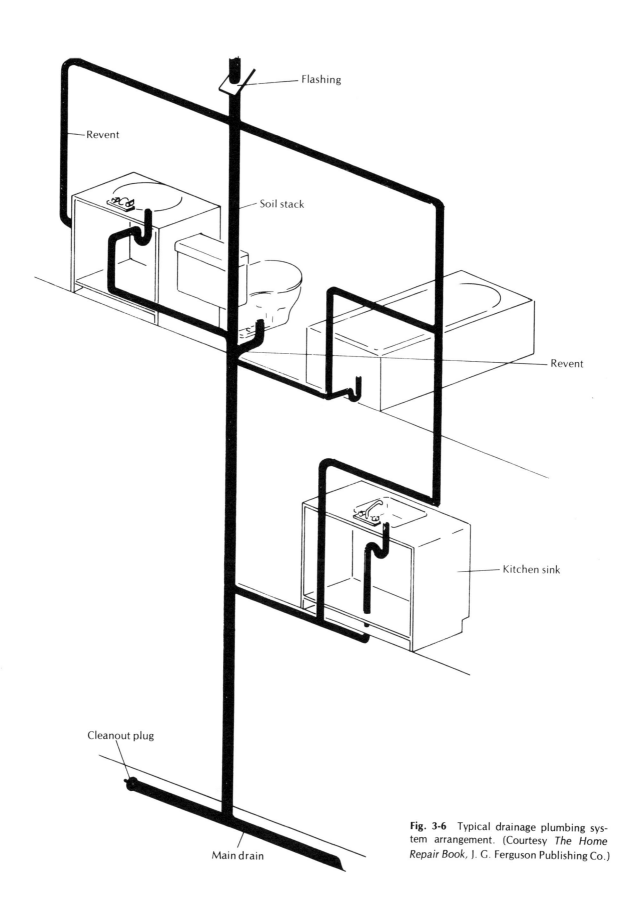

Flashing

Revent

Soil stack

Revent

Kitchen sink

Cleanout plug

Main drain

Fig. 3-6 Typical drainage plumbing system arrangement. (Courtesy *The Home Repair Book*, J. G. Ferguson Publishing Co.)

General Information

Horizontal pipes for the waste system should slope at the rate of ¼" per foot (so that water does not stand, or separate from matter too quickly). Water-supply piping should also slope so that it can be drained.

Piping for waste systems (toilets) is usually 3" to 4" in diameter and thus more easily installed in outside walls where 2 x 6 or 2 x 8 uprights are used for framing. Other drainage pipes (for sinks, showers, tubs, etc.) are usually 3" diameter. These sizes will accomodate almost any house unless your home is a hotel.

Cast iron pipe is excellent for outdoor, underground installations and main soil or waste stacks. Brass piping is expensive and not used a great deal nowadays. Steel pipe is used for supply and drainage systems, but not underground. Copper piping or tubing is used extensively for both water supply and drainage and has become almost standard everywhere because it is easy to handle. Plastic piping is used for outdoor sprinkler systems and swimming pools but often prohibited for hot-water systems and behind-wall installations.

Rigid copper pipe is available in three wall thicknesses: Type M or thick wall, Type L or medium wall, Type K or thin wall. Copper tubing is made only in Types L and K. Fittings can be soldered to both types of tubing.

Plumbing fixtures of all types are readily available today, so there is little need to try to fabricate them. Many building-supply, home-center, and hardware stores stock the different types: T's, T's with side inlets, bends, adapters, Y's, toilet-connecting flanges, couplings, elbows, cleanouts, and unions.

Cutting Pipe

When cutting into pipelines, support the pipe on both sides of the cut. This includes vertical pipes (risers), which need to be supported above and below the cut with metal straps attached to studs and/or joists.

Cast Iron Pipe. Cast iron pipe is available with or without a hub. Hubless types butt together; hub types accommodate the next section in the same manner as male-female fittings. To cut cast iron pipe, mark the pipe at the desired length, making the mark completely around the pipe's circumference. Cut 1/16" deep with a hacksaw, then place the pipe on a block and cold chisel it while turning the pipe until it breaks.

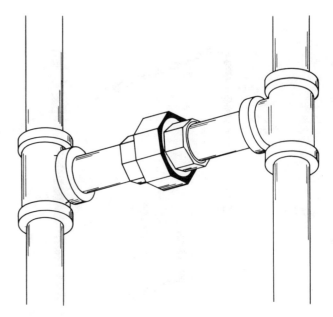

Fig. 3-7   A union is easily made to join two pipes or to install a connecting tee.

To join hub pipe fit the next section into the hub and force and force oakum into the hub to within 1" of the top. You will then need to pour molten lead around the joint. (Local codes specify the amount to be used.) *Molten lead can be dangerous because of splattering. Wear heavy-duty gloves, safety glasses and faceshield, and protective clothing.*

Hubless piping is joined by aligning and butting the ends, and then clamping a rubber or neoprene seal over both pipes and securing the seal with gaskets and clamps.

Steel Pipe.   The number and diversity of fittings available today has eliminated much of the pipe threading and fitting once needed. In most cases, buying and installing two short lengths of threaded-end pipe and installing a union (or other fitting) is fast and simple.

A union (Fig. 3–7) consists of three separate parts: (1) an internally and externally threaded nut, (2) an internally threaded nut, and (3) a larger nut that fits over (1) and (2). The threaded nuts are first screwed onto the two pipe ends and then joined by the larger nut. Joint compound is applied to the external pipe threads and the union. The union is first hand-tightened and then secured using two pipe wrenches.

Copper Piping and Tubing.   Copper piping and tubing has the advantages of being easy to cut, bend, and solder. Cuts should be made using a

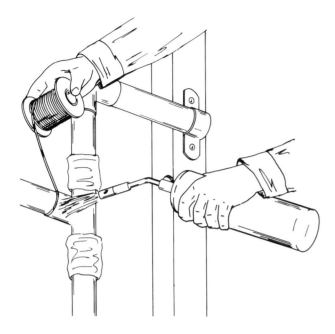

Fig. 3-8 Soldering two lengths of copper tubing using a propane torch.

miter to make sure they are straight. The ends should be polished shiny using sandpaper or steel wool (and wiped to remove grit or other foreign material from inside the tube). Apply a light coat of flux to the end of the pipe and inside the fitting.

Using a propane torch, heat around the entire pipe and fitting joint until it is hot enough to melt solder. Apply solder, letting it flow into the joint until a small ridge appears as shown in Fig. 3–8.

Caution: Do not hold pipe or fitting by hand while soldering. Follow instructions for using propane torch.

Like steel piping, rigid copper pipe can also be fitted with unions and many other fittings readily available at plumbing, building supply, and hardware retail outlets.

If building regulations permit you to make plumbing installations, or if no regulations apply, draw a rough plan before starting the addition. Check all dimensions carefully before installing piping and fixtures, being especially careful to support wall-mounted fixtures (i.e., sink, toilet tank) by nailing supports between the uprights.

Be sure to allow a ¼" slope per foot toward ground level for drainage piping. Allow approximately the same degree of slope for water-supply piping away from ground level (however, the degree of slope may depend on the water pressure).

Installing risers beside an outside wall is usually more convenient than installing them against inside walls. But be sure to insulate behind the pipes in cold climates. Always lay out piping to run in the shortest, most direct lines—making bends and corners only when necessary. And always group the fixtures to simplify the piping layout. Otherwise, you'll spread piping all over the floor, creating a messy layout that will be difficult for you or anyone else to alter or repair.

ELECTRICITY/WIRING

Now that you've laid down temporary subflooring and erected partitions, you'll want to begin work on the lighting fixtures, electrical outlets, and wiring.

You should know that electricity can be dangerous if you don't know what you are doing. Worse off are folks who think they know but don't. No one yet has eliminated all the hazards capable of causing electrical shock and fires. Check with the local building inspector if you plan to make changes or additions to your present electrical system.

Most towns and cities have electrical codes, or have adopted the National Electrical Code, and prohibit electrical work without a permit. The reason for these regulations is to protect you, your family, and your neighbors. You could violate the law if you make alterations and additions without a permit. Many codes are stringent, prohibiting any kind of electrical work except the most minor, like changing a switch. The insurance on your home, furnishings, and personal property could be affected if an electrical fire occurs as a result of your work.

Always make sure the electric power is turned off before you begin work. If you are not sure that it is turned off for the circuit on which you plan to work, then turn if off for the entire house.

Here is a good place to review some basic electrical safety rules:

1. Check with your building inspector before you make wiring changes or additions.

2. Make sure the power is turned OFF and stays off while you are working. (Make a large sign lettered DO NOT TOUCH—DAD'S WORKING, and hang it in front of the main power panel.)

3. Replace fuses with the *correct* size, which doesn't always mean replacing with the same size.

INSTALLING WIRING IN A NEW ROOM

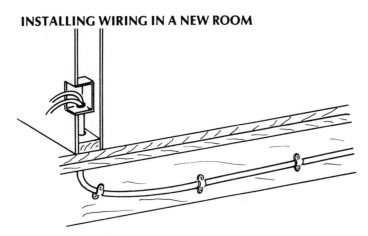

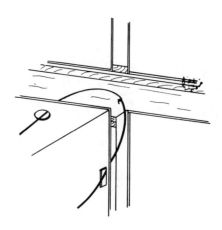

Staple cable to joist using wide electrical staples. Avoid sharp corners or bends. (Courtesy *The Home Repair Book*, J. G. Ferguson Publishing Co.)

To fish a cable from wall through ceiling opening requires a fishhook and patience. (Courtesy *The Home Repair Book*, J. G. Ferguson Publishing Co.)

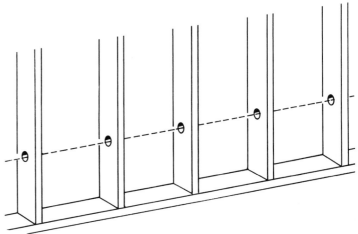

Evenly line up holes for cable runs. Measure distance from floorplate so cable doesn't hump up and down. (Courtesy *The Home Repair Book*, J. G. Ferguson Publishing Co.)

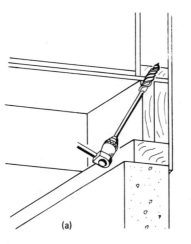

(a)

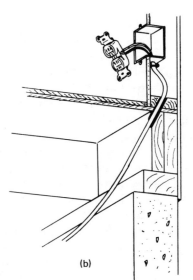

(b)

To run a connection from one floor to another (a) bore hole through floorplate using an augur, and (b) fish cable through to new receptacle. (Courtesy *The Home Repair Book*, J. G. Ferguson Publishing Co.)

CITY OF NEWTON
PUBLIC BUILDINGS DEPARTMENT
Application for Electric Permit

Ser. No. . . . .

Per. No. . . . .

Newton, Mass., ... , 19 . . . .

To the PUBLIC BUILDINGS COMMISSIONER : —

The undersigned hereby applies for a permit to install electric wiring according to the following specifications :

1. Street and No. ?. . . . . .Ward ?. . . . .
2. Nearest cross street ?. . . . .
3. Old or New Building ?. . . . . .Purpose of Building ?. . . . .
4. Owner ?. . . . . .Address ?. . . . .
5. Electrical Contractor :. . . . . .Address :. . . . .
6. How many families ?. . . . . .Estimated Cost :. . . . .
7. Are fixtures which are to be installed ADDITIONAL. . . . . .or REPLACEMENT. . . . .

PROPOSED FIXTURES IN DETAIL

Location of Room	Light Outlets	Sw.	Plugs	Fixt.	Location of Room	Light Outlets	Sw.	Plugs	Fixt.

No. of outlets		Air Conditioner	Rating in amperes
No. of fixtures		Gas Heating	
No. of motors	H.P.	Electric Heating	
No. of signs	Trans.	Oil burner	
Misc.		Range	Rating
Type of Heat -	Forced Hot Water	Water heater	Rating
	" " Air	Clothes dryer	Rating
	Gravity	Total load	
	Steam	Size of main entrance switch	
		Size of service cond. uctor	
		Size of Service Conduit	

ALL WORK HEREAFTER PERFORMED MUST BE TESTED AND THE INSPECTOR MUST BE NOTIFIED WHEN ALL CONNECTIONS THEREWITH ARE PLACED IN POSITION.

Application must be signed by an Electrician only.
Permit must be conspicuously posted on premises before work is commenced.

The above is subscribed to and executed by me under the penalties of perjury in accordance with Chapter 187, Acts of 1926.

Phone number, ... Signature, ...

License number, ... Address, ...

Master, ...

Journeyman, ...

Typical municipal permit required before installing electrical wiring. Cost of permit is nominal, safer than running the risk of electrical hazards or having work rejected by housing inspector.

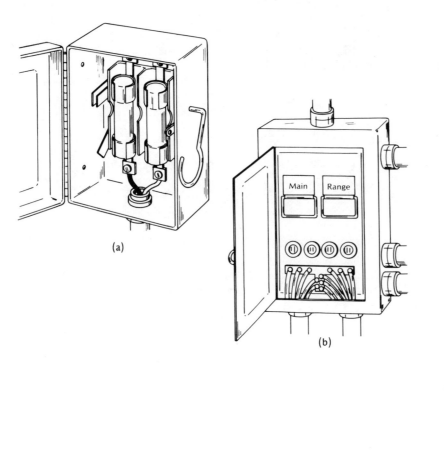

Fig. 3-9 Typical control panels (l-r): (a) fuse box or lever type, (b) drawer type, (c) circuit breaker.

4. Do *not* touch bare or frayed wires or any metal touching them while the power is on.

5. Do *not* touch appliances, fixtures, or switches when you are wet or standing on wet ground.

6. *Never* add fixtures and outlets beyond the capacity of the individual circuit(s). *How to determine the capacity of the different circuits is described on page* 43.

7. Unplug electrical tools (saws, sanders, drills, etc.) after you use them and don't leave them unattended.

8. Make sure the fixtures, switches, etc. have the Underwriters Laboratory (UL) seal on them, which means they are designed and made to approved safety standards.

9. When in doubt, consult a licensed electrician. Doing so can be less costly and less painful.

To Shut Off Power

Your house has (or should have) a control or main power panel or box located where electric power enters the house (the "service entrance"). This enables you to turn power off and on for the entire house, although some houses may have more than one control panel.

There are three basic types of panels, as shown in Fig. 3–9.

1. The "fuse box" or lever type is found in older houses. To shut off electricity, pull the lever down (unless there are other instructions). The door of the panel should not open until all power is shut off.

2. The drawer type is more common today. It usually has two drawers. Pulling out one shuts off the electricity to the range or stove. Pulling

out the other shuts off power to the main electrical circuit, and is the one you should pull out. Drawers should be marked "Main" and "Range" (or other major appliance). Make sure you know which is which.

3. The circuit breaker panel is also very common. This type of panel usually has one or two large switches. To shut off power, push the switch for the main electrical circuit to OFF. Again, if there are two switches, make sure you know which is which.

The first step *before* doing any electrical work is to find out which circuit you will be using. To find the proper circuit,

1. Shut off the electricity at the main power panel.
2. Remove one fuse, or turn one switch to OFF in the case of a circuit breaker.
3. Turn on the power at the panel.
4. Using a small lamp, or better still an electric circuit tester, check all fixtures and outlets (also called receptacles) to determine which fixtures and outlets are "out"—i.e., have no power.
5. List the locations (bedroom, living room, etc.) on a label opposite the fuse or switch.
6. Shut off the main power panel.
7. Replace fuse or push switch (step 2 above) to ON.
8. Remove another fuse (or push another switch).
9. Turn on main power panel.

Repeat this process, taking all nine steps, until you know exactly which fixtures and outlets are on each circuit or line. The electric range, requiring 220 volts, should be on the circuit marked "Range" and doesn't require checking. The same is true of other major appliances such as central air conditioning.

Now that you know which fixtures and outlets are on which circuits, you may want to know whether you can add fixtures or outlets to the line(s) running into the attic, or whether you'll have to connect to circuits in downstairs rooms or even run a separate line to the main power panel. Years ago, many houses had only a basic two-wire power system which provided 30-amp or 3600-watt service. These systems are inadequate, because of the increasing load of electrical appliances. If your house still has this system, the chances of adding fixtures and outlets are not good. You'll only blow fuses and create other problems, some potentially serious.

Most houses today are (or should be) provided wth 115-volt and 230-volt service. (Voltages of 110-220 were once common and 120-240 often used. The National Electric Code now requires determinants based on 115 volts and 230 volts.) These are three-wire systems providing 60-amp, 14,400-watt service or 100-amp, 24,400-watt service.

The circuits you checked are general-purpose circuits. Each has a 15-amp fuse or circuit breaker. It uses No. 14 wire, has a 115-volt rating, and

Appliance	Approx. Wattage Used	Number	Total Watts
Air Conditioner	800–1600	_____	_____
Lights			
Fluorescent	15–60	_____	_____
Incandescent	10–300	_____	_____
Clock	2	_____	_____
Electric Blanket	200	_____	_____
Radio (portable)	50	_____	_____
Stereo Hi-fi	300	_____	_____
Television			
Black and White	250	_____	_____
Color	300	_____	_____
		Total:	_____

maximum capacity of about 1750 watts. Or, each has a 20–amp circuit, uses No. 12 wire, and has 2300–watts capacity for small kitchen appliances (toasters, broilers, etc.) and home workshop tools. The existing circuit(s) in your attic will most likely be the No. 14 wire, 15–amp type, capable of supplying 1750 watts.

Whether or not it will handle additional fixtures and outlets depends on whether you intend to install a simple light fixture or a one-ton air conditioner.

Now you need to know the electrical usage on the circuit or line. The sample table of the wattages used by different appliances will help you make that determination.

Figuring the total requires common sense as well as the ability to add. For one thing, the figures shown above are maximum wattage requirements. Today, most of us rarely turn on a 300-watt bulb. We use 60-, 75- or 100-watt bulbs and don't turn them on any earlier than we must. So, don't figure you're using 1800 watts because you have six lamps plugged into the circuit. The total may be considerably less because all six are seldom used at the same time.

The other side of the coin is that the circuit could be a very active one. Suppose you have a color TV, stereo, and four 150-watt bulbs being used at the same time, for a total of 1200 watts. If you are planning to use another color TV, stereo, and two 300-watt bulbs in the upstairs room on the same line, you have problems.

Similarly, if you intend to install a one-ton room air conditioner in the upstairs for hot weather use, you are looking at a major electrical project. Running a new line to the central power panel is work for a licensed electrician.

Before making changes or additions, make a plan: a simple diagram showing the locations of new fixtures, outlets, and switches, and roughly where the cable(s) will need to run.

Following are examples of work you may be able to perform. But check with your building or wiring inspector.

To Extend Wiring from One Outlet or Box to Another

1. Shut off power for the circuit and make sure it stays off. (Post sign previously described.)
2. Pull out electrical fixture. Handle it gently, don't yank it from the wall.

3. Remove knockout from existing outlet box. (Knock out the cap facing in the direction the new electrical cable will run.) See Fig. 3–10.
4. Run cable to new outlet securing it along the way with insulated staples.
5. Strip ½" of insulation from wire ends of cable and connect to existing outlet, black wire to black wire and white to white.

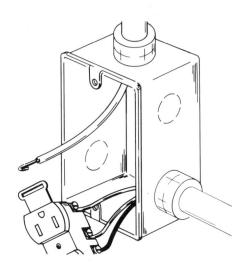

Fig. 3-10 Knock out cap facing the direction in which cable will run.

6. Strip 6" of insulation from other end of cable.
7. Slip cable connector over wires and cable and fasten.
8. Connect wires to new electrical outlet and attach ground.
9. Restore electric power and check your work.

To Add a Switch Beyond a Light at the End of a Circuit

1. Shut off power.
2. Remove light fixture from its location.
3. Disconnect wires.
4. Strip ½" of insulation from wires in cable to be installed.
5. Insert wires in connectors, black to black and white to white.
6. Run cable to new switch location, securing it with insulated staples.
7. Strip ½" of insulation from wires in cable.

EXTERIOR OUTLET

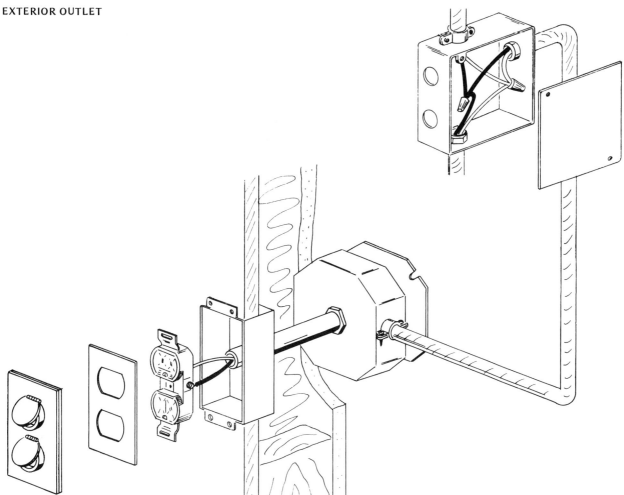

Typical hookup and line for outside lighting fixture. This is the time to ensure that you have connections for outdoor Christmas lights or the security of external flood lights for the dark areas of your yard. (Courtesy *The Home Repair Book*, J. G. Ferguson Publishing Co.)

8. Slip connector over cable and fasten.
9. Attach wires to switch and ground.
10. Install switch.
11. Restore electric power and check your work.

To Install a New Lighting Fixture

Installing a new lighting fixture is similar to installing a new outlet. As you work on your project, installing new fixtures may be more convenient than using extension cords and lights. The fixtures are easily put in place, and can be removed when necessary to wallboard or panel around them, and then reinstalled. Remember: fluorescent lighting provides more light at less cost than incandescent lighting and also saves energy.

1. Shut off power.

2. Pull out electrical fixture or junction box that will transmit power to the next fixture. (Handle fixtures and wires gently.)

3. Remove knockout from outlet box, selecting knockout facing in direction you intend to run the cable. If connection is being made from a junction box, disconnect wires and insert into connectors.

4. Strip ½" of insulation from wire ends of cable and fasten to outlet. If making connection to a junction box, strip ½" of insulation from cable and insert wires in connectors, black to black, and white to white.

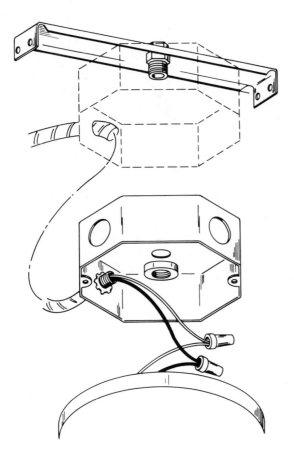

Fig. 3-11 Drawing shows components, installation of a typical lighting fixture.

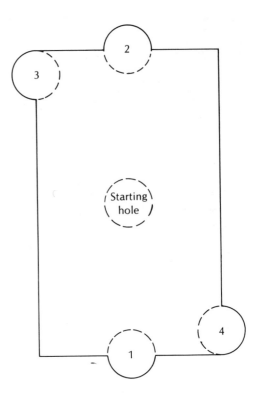

Fig. 3-12 Procedure for cutting a hole for an electrical outlet or switch.

5. Run cable to new lighting fixture location, securing cable along the way with insulated staples.

6. Strip 6" of insulation from ends of wires.

7. Slip connector over wires and cable and fasten.

8. Install chassis for fluorescent fixture. (Fig. 3–11) Sockets, ballasts, and wiring are mounted on the fixture. Do not insert tube until fixture is positioned. Position fixture below outlet box so that stud(s) or bolt(s) poke through chassis. Tighten chassis. Connect wires, black to black, and white to white.

9. Incandescent and circline fixtures are installed in the same manner except that some use a metal plate or strap rather than a chassis (sometimes called a pan). Slip the plate over the stud or bolt first, then tighten using a locknut. Fixture is installed over the plate.

10. Connect black to black wires, and white to white, to the fixture using connectors.

11. Install fixture.

12. Restore power and check your work.

Lighting fixtures are usually located overhead or on walls where they will provide the best lighting for reading, sewing, etc. Switches are located 4' above the floor and outlets (also called "receptacles"; 12" above the floor and 8"-12" above counters.

Fig. 3–12 shows the sequence to cut holes in walls for electrical outlets and switches. Draw an outline using an actual box. Drill starter hole in the center of outline if wall is of plaster–and–lath construction. Then enlarge hole leaving ample space on the laths to attach the outlet. If the wall is drywall construction, drill starter holes in center and at points 1, 2, 3, and 4 and then cut around the outline using a keyhole saw. Since the outlet will need to be supported and attached, locate it beside a stud.

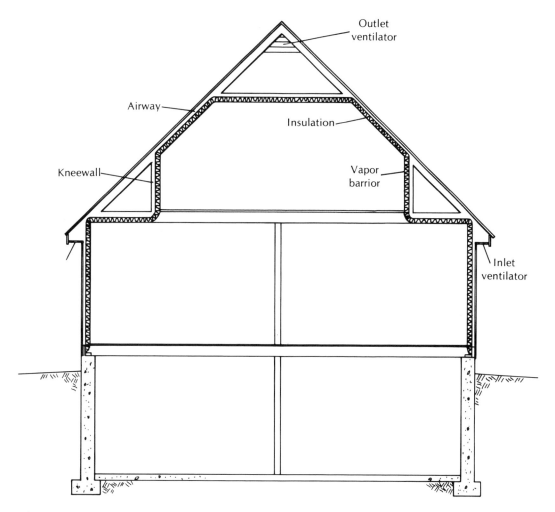

Fig. 3-13   Plan to insulate behind the kneewalls before finishing the attic. (Courtesy USDA)

INSULATING THE ATTIC

Finishing an attic area without providing adequate insulation doesn't make sense today.

Fuel costs—whether for electricity, oil, gas, coal, or wood—have already doubled and tripled. The long-term forecasts are highly unfavorable. Experts believe the world's supply of oil will begin a long, slow decline during the 1990s and oil and gas will become increasingly scarce and expensive. Coal will be available but expensive to mine, and burning it will present new pollution problems. In the meantime, your well-built home could last fifty, one hundred, or many more years.

Some other points: almost anyone can insulate. You don't need a permit or license. And once the job is done the insulation will last for years. You'll recover the costs of insulating in reduced fuel bills within a few years, and at the same time add permanent value to your home.

Fig. 3-13 shows the areas where a house should be insulated. If there is a garage below a living area then the walls and roof of the garage must also be insulated. If there is no insulation, or very little, in the walls, insulation must be blown in by a contractor using special equipment. If your house does not have a basement, installing rolls or batts of insulation between the crawl space and the subfloor may be possible, but it's a back-breaking job.

Note, especially, that insulation is installed behind the kneewalls to provide further protection and comfort. Isolating the waste or storage space may obviate the need to install a radiator or air conditioner in a new upstairs room.

Insulating the Ceiling

Because heat rises, insulating the ceiling is critical for heating. The amount of insulation needed depends on the climate or temperature zone in which you live.

Insulation in rolls or batts is available with or without foil facing. Foil-faced insulation costs about $1 more per roll, but reflects heat (cool air during summer) back toward the living area. Unfaced insulation can be installed, but a vapor barrier (usually polyethylene sheeting), should be installed between the unfaced insulation and the living area.

You can add insulation over existing insulation, but if you use the foil-faced types over old insulation, slash the new foil-faced insulation with a knife (or remove the foil) to let moisture vapor pass through. Working with the foil-faced types is easier because they have stapling edges and there is no need to add a polyethylene vapor barrier.

R-numbers are used as a measure of resistance to winter heat loss or summer heat gain. These numbers also indicate the thickness of the insulation.

R-number	Thickness
R-11	3" to 4"
R-13	3½" to 3 5/8"
R-19	
R-22	5" to 7"

Ideally, insulating batts or rolls of about 6" thickness should be installed between the rafters, collar beams, sloping rafters, and in dormer ceilings. However, in many cases, the depth of the rafters or studs is insufficient to accommodate 6"-thick insulation. In those places, 3"- or 4"-thick insulation must be used.

To determine how much insulation you'll need, calculate the quantity by measuring the area to be covered: length multiplied by width. If the rafters are 16" apart, multiply the total by 0.90. If the rafters are 24" apart, multiply the total by 0.94. The answer will give you the total number of square feet you need.

Be sure to notice the distance between the rafters. Most insulation today is manufactured in rolls or batts 15" or 23" wide; 19" insulation is sometimes available but becoming increasingly difficult to obtain. In addition to a tape measure, you'll need a straightedge to cut along. (A 3'-long

Fig. 3-14   Start the insulation at the highest points in the attic. (Courtesy Project Conserve)

board will also do the job.) You'll need a sharp knife to cut the batts or rolls and a staple gun and staples to attach the insulation. (½" heavy-duty staples are recommended.)

Start by stapling the insulation through the border or margin available on most insulating rolls to the sides of the rafters at the highest points in your attic as shown in Fig. 3-14.

Staple the roll about halfway between the roof deck and the rafter edge, leaving two or three inches on each side of the insulation to entrap the air. (This air space is important.) Using 6"-thick insulation may not provide ample space for the air trap which is one reason why you may need to use a thinner roll or batt. Even then, it may not be possible to leave even ½" or 1" of air space on each side of the roll. Incidentally, trying to install insulation upward from the bottom of a sloping roof is difficult. Start at the top.

Install the foil or vapor shield side of the insulation toward the living area. If you use unfaced insulation that has no foil, you will need to cover the entire area with a separate vapor barrier. See Fig. 3-15.

Slowly unroll the insulation, working downward, stapling it on each side to the rafter or stud. Space the staples about 6" apart.

Cover the entire area between the rafters until you reach the bottom of the eaves. If your eaves overhang the house, do *not* extend the insulation outward. Instead, tuck the insulation into the space beneath the attic floor and the ceiling of the room below.

Wear gloves, long-sleeve shirt when installing insulation to prevent skin irritations. (Courtesy American Optical Corporation)

Wearing safety goggles and hard hat when hammering nails, working under beams can help prevent eye injuries, painful bumps and bruises. (Courtesy American Optical Corporation)

Slip on a faceshield or safety goggles when you use power tools to protect yourself from flying slivers. (Courtesy American Optical Corporation)

Fig. 3-15 Install a vapor barrier if you use unfaced insulation. Courtesy Project Conserve)

To make the installation permanent, you should support the insulation by stringing wire under the rolls or batts. Chickenwire will also support the insulation and keep it in place, preventing it from sagging. The chickenwire can be stapled to the sides of the rafters and studs just as you stapled the insulation. However, you will probably need to cut the chickenwire to fit between the rafters, using pliers or a wire cutter.

If you have odd-shape ceiling areas—places that are cut into because of chimneys, dormers, turrets, or towers—you must cut odd shapes of insulation and install them to fit. This cutting will eliminate the stapling edge or the margin of the insulation. When that occurs, add a stapling edge by using tape or pull out some of the insulation and staple through the vapor barrier.

Some Do's and Don'ts

Don't insulate over eave and gable vents. In winter, they let moisture escape. In summer, the moving air reduces heat build-up.

Don't insulate over a recessed lighting fixture or motors. Make a shield from a metal can to hold the insulation at least 3" away from the fixture or motor.

Do handle electrical wires and cables with care; refrain from bending them as much as possible.

Do wear work gloves and a long-sleeve shirt when you are handling insulation. The fibers can sometimes cause skin irritations.

Do wear safety goggles to protect your eyes when stapling, hammering, or working in dusty places.

Do watch out for protruding nails, especially those above your head. Wear a safety hat or bump cap to protect yourself from bumps and bruises.

Do wear a mask to avoid inhaling fibers.

Do wear eye protection when using power tools.

Insulating the Walls

If your attic has walls or kneewalls, they should also be insulated. The procedure is very similar to insulating the roof. R-19, or 5"- to 8"-thick, insulation should be used when possible. If not, use a lower R number. Whatever you use, insulate before completing your project, because the likelihood of fuel costs coming down is minimal.

To insulate a wall, simply fit the end of a roll (sometimes precut batts of the exact length are available) against the top plate or piece of framing. Working down, staple the border or flange on the side of the roll to the sides of the studs. If necessary, you can staple them to the faces of the studs. Space should be left between the insulation and the outer wall as an air trap or block.

Space the staples approximately 6" to 8" apart. Cut the roll to fit tightly against the framing at the bottom (the bottom plate or shoe). When you butt the ends of two rolls in a single stud space, butt them tightly so that warm air can't escape through the gap.

If some of the spaces between the studs are narrower than the insulation, cut the insulation about 1" wider than the space to be filled. Staple the remaining flange and then pull the foil over to

Fig. 3-16 Hand-stuff small spaces with loose insulation. (Courtesy Project Conserve)

Insulate waste space with insulating rolls or batts to keep heat in during winter, cool air in summer. (Courtesy Certainteed Corporation)

the other side and staple through the barrier or foil into the stud.

Unfaced insulation can also be used to insulate a wall and a separate vapor barrier stretched over the entire surface. The barrier can be either 2-mil-thick polyethylene sheeting or foil-backed wallboard. Pull the polyethylene sheeting taut while stapling it in place.

Install insulation behind pipes, ducts, electrical conduit, and boxes by hand-packing the area with loose pieces of insulation pulled from a roll.

To insulate around windows, hand-stuff the narrow spaces with loose insulation and cover them with a strip of foil or vapor barrier. See Fig. 3–16.

Insulating the Floor

You may or may not decide to insulate the attic floor. Doing so will help keep the downstairs rooms warm in winter and cool in summer, but make the attic room cold in winter, hot in summer.

You have four choices: (1) insulate and install a heating system with separate thermostat in the attic room; (2) insulate and heat the room with portable heaters and fans as needed; (3) do not insulate the floor allowing heat from the downstairs room to flow up to the attic in the winter, and cool air in summer; and (4) insulate over the waste space in the attic.

Pour loose-fill vermiculite insulation be-tween joists for maximum insulation and energy savings. (Courtesy W. R. Grace & Co., Construction Products Division)

If you decide to insulate the whole floor or just under the waste space, you can use one or a combination of several methods.

1. Lay unfaced insulation over the old insulation, fitting it snugly against the joist as shown in photo on page 51.
2. Lay insulation over the old insulation. If you use foil-faced insulation, remember to slash it with a knife to allow moisture to pass through. Unfaced insulation is less expensive than foil-faced insulation but you may not always find unfaced insulation in stock.
3. Pour vermiculite or mineral wool over the old insulation and level it with a board or rake.

Loose, free-flowing vermiculite or mineral wool is also very useful for filling in around pipes and electrical conduit, rather than piecing to-gether bits of fiberglas insulation. When using vermiculite or mineral wool, pour it to the height of the joists and then level it with a board. See photo above.

Remember, if you are planning to install new electrical outlets, or change the locations of exist-ing units, you will find it more convenient to do the electrical work before insulating. The same applies to plumbing installations.

Another pointer: insulating material should be fluffy, not compacted, in order to entrap the air passing through. Fluff up insulation, don't press it down.

Windows/Storm Windows

Attic windows, especially, should be equipped with storm windows. Heat rises but also escapes to the sides. You should install double- or triple-pane windows or combination storm-screen alu-minum windows. Caulk around the edges of the frames to retain heat during winter, cool air during summer.

Do not close up the attic vents, usually located at opposite sides of the area. A certain amount of free-flowing air is needed to prevent moisture and condensation within your home.

Insulation Costs

Insulating materials are no longer inexpensive, but there are no cheap substitutes. In the old days, newspapers were often used but are no longer recommended. They can get wet, heavy, and odorous. There is also a possibility of rodents and other vermin nesting in the walls. Materials such as fiberglass, vermiculite, and mineral wool are free of such problems.

Further information about insulating is readily available from building supply and hardware dealers, many electric and gas utilities, and from appropriate federal, state. and municipal agencies.

4

FINISHING THE UPSTAIRS

Now that you have roughed in the partitions, and had the wiring and plumbing connections installed, you'd like to start the finishing work. And why not? Seeing the fruits of your labor is always a gratifying experience.

Before you started, you decided whether to panel from the eaves to the peak or to paint and decorate what is now becoming an upstairs room instead of a gloomy and perhaps untidy attic area.

Incidentally, you may find disagreements as to what stage of the finishing job should be completed next: ceiling, walls, or floor. The next step depends on your plan and common sense. If you intend to have drywall construction, using wallboard or gypsumboard, you should do the ceiling first. On the other hand, you may plan to panel from the eaves to the peak. In that case, you might finish the floor first. But if you intend to lay carpeting or floor tile you will certainly want to complete any dirty work before tile, rug or even tongue–and–groove flooring is installed.

The attic ceiling may need to be framed using 2 x 4's for joists. Or, as some of the photographs in this book suggest, you may let the roof of the house become a kind of natural ceiling, which is a good idea where headspace is limited.

DRYWALL CONSTRUCTION

Drywall, as opposed to plaster, can mean one of several different but similar materials: wallboard, gypsumboard, sheetrock, fiberboard, hardboard, and plywood.

The material described here is one of the first three: wallboard, gypsumboard, or sheetrock. It is lightweight, fire resistant, relatively sturdy, and inexpensive (about $3 per 4' x 8' sheet or panel). It is easy to install, and when properly installed should provide good service for many years.

A wallboard ceiling should be installed before erecting the walls in order to assure a tight, snug fit. The same material can be used for ceilings or walls, and painted or papered after it is primed. The wallboard provides sturdy backing and support for lightweight, prefinished panels, and is usually installed horizontally rather than vertically when erecting walls. The 1/2" and 5/8" thicknesses are recommended. Handling these panels is a 2–person job, one supporting the panel while the other hammers in the nails.

As previously mentioned, partitions leave waste space between the wall and roof. Refer to Chapter 3 and insulate behind the wallboard using 3½"–thick insulation with the foil side facing toward the living area. New types of wallboard are now available that offer additional insulation.

Wallboard can also be installed on both sides of the partition, placing the insulation between the sheets. Double layers are sometimes used in order to provide increased fire resistance, sound absorption, strength, and durability.

As much as possible, use the full size of the 4' x 8' wallboard sheets to avoid cutting and trimming. This can be accomplished by starting in corners. To cut wallboard, score the cutting line with a utility knife. Move the line over the edge of a table and set a board along the table side of the line. Then snap the wallboard. Getting a sharp, clean cut takes practice, so experiment with a few unusable pieces. You may find using a saber or jig saw with a special wallboard–cutting blade more effective. Sand and smooth the rough edges of the sheet.

You can attach wallboard to studs using nails, screws or special–purpose adhesives. The adhesives may be neater, but nailing is less expensive (or can be, depending on your skill).

The nails recommended are 1 1/4" to 1 3/4" long, flat headed (1/4" to 5/16" diameter) and annular threaded for greater holding power. In the single–nail system, nails are hammered 7" apart into the walls and 8" apart into the ceiling. Double–nailing involves locating nails about 12" apart and then nailing a second row, each nail being located about 2" away from the first row. Double–nailing is used when the boards seem loose and firmer contact is needed. Nails should be driven straight and centered into the joists and uprights. To allow for normal expansion and contraction of the wallboard, do not nail closer than within 7" of the ceiling and 8" of the wall when walls and ceilings abut. Nails should always be hammered in carefully to avoid fracturing the finish.

The screws used in drywall construction have Phillips type heads. They should be long enough to penetrate at least 3/8" to 5/8" into joists, studs, and supports. Directions for applying adhesives are provided with the adhesives and should be followed closely. Their use may depend on the temperature and climate of the area in which you live. Proper installation of drywall is essential because otherwise the sheets can loosen, pop out, and bulge, ruining the appearance of the room. (Remember, you'll want the room to look good for many years and not have to redo your work next spring or the following year.)

After you have nailed the drywall panels in place, you'll notice a problem: namely, those spaces between the sheets and the indentations of the nailheads will show when you paint the room. You'll need to tape the joints and cover the tape and nailheads. Start by filling the joints with an embedding compound, using a broad–blade knife to flatten and "feather" around the joints. Apply the tape, centering and smoothing it to prevent wrinkling. Use a knife to remove excessive compound.

The tape and compound will most likely leave a rough surface that must be sanded, and a second light coat of compound and tape applied. This step may need to be repeated two or three times in order to obtain the smooth–as–silk surface necessary if you plan to paint the room.

Automatic taping machines are available for single–step filling and taping. If you borrow or rent a machine, practice using it until you can handle it efficiently.

Finishing compound is applied over the tape. Be careful to remove excess compound. Each coat should dry thoroughly before applying the next coat.

The exposed wallboard corners will be covered and protected by the trim: wood casings around the window and door frames, baseboards at the floor level, and moldings at the ceiling level. Metal corner beads and casings are used to protect the outsides of difficult–to–tape corners. The metal corner beads, except U–shape types, are crimped into position with a special tool or pair of pliers after the wallboard is installed. U–shape bead must be placed in position before installing the wallboard. The beads must be covered with compound to conceal them and to provide a smooth surface for painting and papering.

Wallboard has some deficiencies as a finishing material, but if problems arise they can usually be corrected. Nails can be removed and replaced with screws. Cracks can be filled. Tape can be sanded down and coated. Ridges may appear, but they too can be sanded before the surface is refinished. The way to avoid these problems is to handle the wallboard smoothly and carefully and hammer each nail without fracturing the wallboard. Because the nails are countersunk, you will get a certain amount of dimpling that is easily covered by compound or tape. But again, avoid breaking or fracturing the wallboard.

If you plan to paint the room, the wallboard will need to be primed and sealed with an emulsion that will close the pores and provide a uniform texture. However, there are many predecorated drywall materials and perhaps you have already selected one of them. With predecorated drywall, special tapes and nails must be purchased, adding to the cost.

PANELING

Paneling has become extremely popular almost everywhere because of its good–looking appearance, and easy installation and maintenance. The variety of woods and finishes is almost unlimited, ranging from simulated knotty pine and maple to exotic woods like bookmatched teak and sliced rosewood. Prices range from a few dollars per 4' x 8' panel to $20 and more.

You can get a rough idea of how much paneling you'll need by figuring four 4' x 8' panels for every 10' of room perimeter and subtracting one-half panel for each door and one–quarter panel for each window. This assumes the finished room

This attic room's walls and ceiling are completely covered with fabric to give it a warm and cozy look. The doors open to a deck over the garage. Design by Shirley Regendahl. (Courtesy Waverly Fabrics)

What an attic area can look like after you've done some not-so-hard work. Wide shelf doubles as desk area. Room designed by Shirley Regendahl. (Courtesy Waverly Fabrics)

will have an 8'-high ceiling. These are rough measurements only. Before you make actual purchases, figure more closely how the panels will fit—where you will need to cut for windows and doors.

The finish of prefinished panels needs to be protected before installation. Handle the panels carefully, so that the finish doesn't become nicked, scuffed, marred, or bruised. Minor marks can be repaired by applying pastes and polishes of the same color but badly-splintered sections may need to be cut out of the panel and new sections fitted into the panel to replace the damaged sections. If the panels must be stored before use, keep them in a dry room. Lay them flat, inserting blocks of soft wood between the panels. Do *not* slide one panel over another. Forty-eight hours before installation, stand the panels in the room in which they will be used to acclimate them to the room's temperature and moisture conditions. You should also arrange the panels in sequence to see how they will look, matching color and grain from one panel to the next.

Many types of paneling can be applied directly to the studs, provided they are properly backed by stringers or supporting studs. You'll probably need to insert at least one stringer, a 2 x 2 or 2 x 4, half-way between the top and bottom plates. If the panels are lightweight, two or more stringers, located one-third and two-thirds the distance between the plates, may need to be inserted. All panel edges and ends must be properly supported. Frequently, 1 3/8"-thick wallboard or 5/16"-thick plywood sheathing is recommended.

This backing may not seem important at the time of installation, but unless your work is first-class you will eventually regret not spending more time doing the initial work properly.

Prefinished paneling can be nailed directly to studs or a backing wall using 1" to 2" thick colored nails. The nails should be countersunk, hammered in so that their heads are slightly below the surface using a punch or nail to recess the nail head in the grooves and the tiny holes filled using a matching color putty stick.

Direct-to-stud nailing requires 6" spacing along the panel edges and ends, and 12" spacing elsewhere, depending on how solid the backing is. Use 2" nails, spacing them 4" to 6" apart when you nail into studs.

Furring strip should be used especially with lightweight panels that are likely to sag or buckle. These are laths or strips of wood, 1–2" wide x 1/4– 1/2" thick and cut to length, which support the

Fig. 4-1 Dropping a plumbline from ceiling to floor before paneling. (Courtesy Georgia-Pacific Corporation)

Chalk line

Fig. 4-2 Checking measurements to determine if panel needs trimming. (Courtesy Georgia-Pacific Corporation)

panel from the back. If furring strips are used, nail about 8" apart along the edges and 16" elsewhere.

Adhesives are also widely used for fastening panels to studs and backing walls. Some do-it-yourself folks find adhesives easier to use than nails. Make sure the wall, studs, and blocks are absolutely clean and free of dust particles. Use a cloth dampened in rubbing alcohol to remove sawdust. Make certain the panel will fit properly before applying the adhesive because some adhesives dry rapidly, making the panels impossible to move.

Fig. 4–1 shows the proper way to begin paneling. Drop a plumbline (or chalkline) from ceiling to floor 4' away from the corner where you plan to

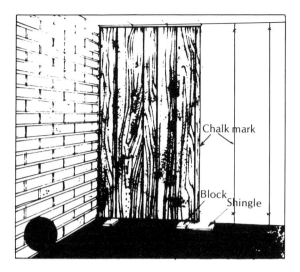

Fig. 4-3 Butt the first panel against the opposing wall. (Courtesy Georgia-Pacific Corporation)

Fig. 4-5 Scribing with a compass to transfer contour from wall to panel. (Courtesy Georgia-Pacific Corporation)

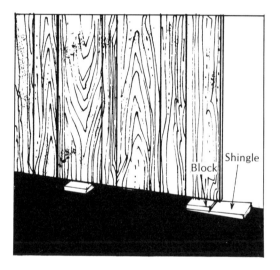

Fig. 4-4 Use a shingle or small block of wood to hold panel in position. (Courtesy Georgia-Pacific Corporation)

begin paneling. Then drop three others, about 1' apart, as shown in Fig. 4–2. Measure tne distances to determine if you need to trim the panel, as in the case of a ceiling or floor that isn't quite level.

Butt the first panel against the perpendicular–opposing wall, as shown in Fig. 4–3. Make sure the panel is plumb. The edge of the panel away from the corner must rest against a stud exactly on center: overlap 1" of the 2" side of a 2 x 4. If it doesn't, trim the panel so that is fits on center because the next panel will also need to be fastened to the stud.

Allow 1/2" clearance above and below the panel. These spaces will be concealed later by the

while nailing, insert a shingle or small block of wood under the panel to hold it in place as shown in Fig. 4–4.

Scribing is used to measure short distances around windows, doors, fireplaces, and corners. The tool used is a scribing compass, the same type you used in school to draw arcs and circles. Measure the distance between the last panel and the edge of the window or wall. Transfer the measurement to the panel you are about to cut and mark it, using the pencil in the compass. A good china-marking pencil is recommended. Scribing is especially useful when you need to cut intricate shapes. See Fig. 4–5 for an example of how scribing is performed.

The second panel is then installed. Tap it lightly against the first panel to make sure the two panels butt snugly. This panel, as all the others, must be supported at the bottom by a shingle or small block of wood.

The way to cut a shape for an electrical outlet box is to (1) stand the panel perfectly straight against the wall with the outlet, (2) place a block of soft wood against the panel and perhaps a rag between the block and panel so you don't mar the finish, (3) tap the panel gently but firmly so that the outline of the box is indented on the back of the panel.

Then follow the sequence described for cutting holes for electric switches and outlets (Refer back to Fig. 3–12). (1) Drill a pilot hole in the center of the outline and then pilot holes in the four corners, drilling from the back of the panel,

A small attic area can easily become a convenient overnight guestroom that doesn't require all the amenities. (Courtesy ▶ Velux-America Inc.)

Under the roof becomes a conversation corner lighted by the sun and the moon, or a good place to read. (Courtesy Velux-America Inc.)

Lighted by roof windows, the former attic can become a pleasant living area and perhaps even an apartment. (Courtesy ▶ Velux-America Inc.)

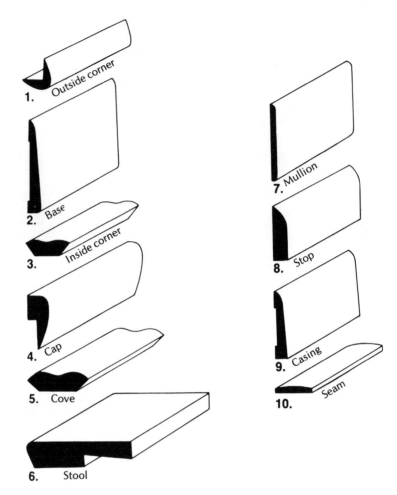

Fig. 4-6   Ten common types of molding or trim. (Courtesy Georgia-Pacific Corporation)

(2) turn the panel over, (3) draw an outline using the circumferences of the holes as the outermost points of the outline, and (4) cut out the panel using a hand keyhole saw or saber saw if you can handle one proficiently. Ragged or splintered edges, if not too severe, will be hidden under the outlet cover or plate.

The kind of saw you use makes a big difference in cutting panels. When using a hand cross–cut saw, cut through the finished side of the panel. Use a fine-tooth saw. If you use a saber saw, cut from the back of the panel. Always use a fine-tooth finish blade and never a rip or coarse blade. Hollow-ground blades, which cut more slowly, should be used with power saws. Also, make sure the panel is firmly supported on two or more saw-horses because excessive vibration will throw off

your cutting line and also cause splintering and fragmenting.

MOLDING AND TRIM

Many different types of moldings, including pre-finished moldings, are readily available. You should purchase them when you purchase paneling, so that you can match colors and grains at the same time. To order molding, measure the estimated distances as closely as possible increasing the amount slightly to allow for molding around corners.

Fig. 4–6 shows the different types of molding: (1) outside corner, (2) base, (3) inside corner, (4) cap, (5) cove, (6) stool, (7) mullion, (8) stop, (9) casing, and (10) seam.

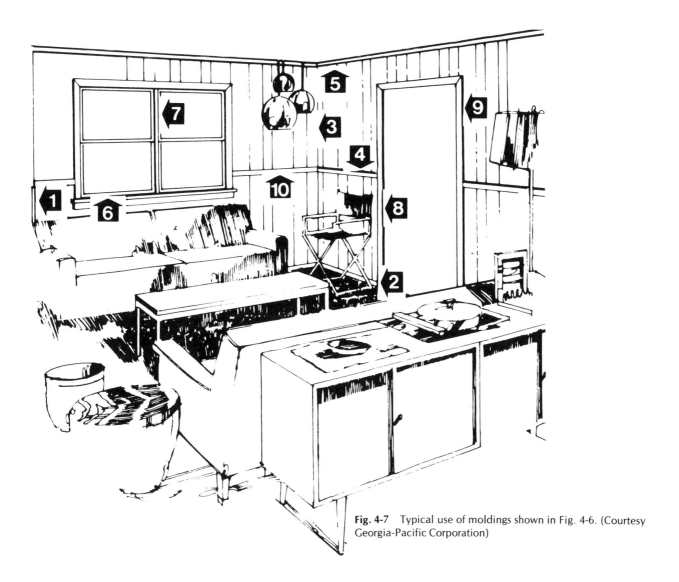

Fig. 4-7 Typical use of moldings shown in Fig. 4-6. (Courtesy Georgia-Pacific Corporation)

Fig. 4–7 shows where these different types of moldings are typically installed, for example, cove at the ceiling, stop beside casing, seam as a dividing line, base at floor level, and so on.

To install molding you will need to make miter cuts using a miter box and a fine–tooth saw. To cut the molding for a corner, cut one piece first at a 45° angle and then cut a second piece from the opposite side at a 45° angle. In general, you can't go wrong if you place the molding in the miter box in the same direction you intend to install it.

Sometimes splicing may be necessary: fitting one section of molding into another. To splice, cut into each section of molding at a 45° angle, again from opposite sides. The spliced parts are then separately mounted and nailed or attached with an adhesive. The nails used are 1″ (2d) finish nails, of the same color as the molding, which have very small heads so that their appearance is not noticeable. You can countersink them by tapping them in lightly using another nail or purchase a special nail set for this purpose. They can also be covered with a matching color putty stick.

Coping makes more professional–looking moldings, the two sections of molding fitting together as though they were molded into one. The profile of one piece will fit into and match the other piece. To make a cope joint, scribe an outline using a small compass or pair of dividers and then cut using a small coping saw. On simple pieces, you can trace the outline of one section on the back of the section to be cut.

PLASTERING

Plastering is an art and craft developed and improved through the centuries. Its use today, however, is limited to more expensive homes. It requires training, experience, and skill; a beginner who does not take the time and trouble to learn the craft can create a mess requiring hours of cleaning and redoing. Perhaps the best advice is to attend a course in plastering or at least read *Plastering Skill and Practice* by F. Van Den Branden and Thomas J. Hartsell, published by the American Technical Society.

Some readers, whose projects involve older houses where there is already plaster and lath construction, might like to know a little more about the subject.

Plaster consists of an aggregate, cementing material, and water. To this mixture are added admixtures: accelerators to speed up the setting time, retarders to slow it down. There are a number of different types of plaster, which vary in composition. Putty coat (which goes by many different names), Keenes cement and Portland cement plaster are probably the most widely used plasters in residential construction because they can be worked into smooth, hard surfaces. All are wet materials that need to be mixed in a trough, although small quantities can be mixed on a table or bench.

The mixture is applied to wood or metal laths, or to entire boards of which some types are perforated. (Gypsumboard laths require a special gypsum mortar.) The once–typical old wood laths are now pretty well standardized in 5/16" x 1 1/2" x 4" sizes. They are nailed to the studs, spacing the laths 3/8" apart and 1/4" between the ends of the lengths. This allows the mortar to flow between the laths and bond itself to them. The laths must be wet before the mortar is applied, otherwise the dry wood will draw moisture from the plaster and weaken the mix.

Two to three coats need to be applied using a trowel. Spreading, compacting, and smoothing the mortar is performed with tools known as a "rod" (a straightedge), "featheredge" (to straighten corners), "darby" (compacts and smooths the mortar), and a "slicker" (similar to a darby).

Each coat of mortar is scratched or roughed before it sets to provide a rough finish to which the second coat can adhere and interlock. The final coat, of course, is smooth unless preferences call for swirls or other design effects. Plaster can also be tinted or colored.

Fig. 4-8   Direct to ceiling installation of ceiling tile.

Plaster surfaces, both interior and exterior, are used in many of the world's most architecturally renowned buildings and homes. As a material, plaster offers the advantages of being strong and hard, and it's a much sturdier material in which to insert picture and portrait hangers and other fasteners. However, unless you are prepared to take the time and trouble to learn this special craft, you will be better off completing your project with other materials.

THE CEILING

While you were making your plans, you should have given some thought to the ceiling as well as the walls. If you decided on a wallboard or gypsumboard ceiling properly painted, then your project is almost complete. Your own painting skills will tell you whether to paint the ceiling before installing the panels.

Perhaps you planned a tile ceiling. Figures 4–8, 4–9 and 4–10 show three different systems of tiling a ceiling: (1) applying the tile directly to the wallboard using an adhesive or mastic, (2) installing a grid system using furring channels and crosstees, and (3) installing a suspended ceiling.

All three make fine–looking ceilings, but the third system, a suspended ceiling, is more often used in basement areas to conceal pipes, ducts,

Fig. 4-9 Ceiling tile or "planks" installed in channels and crosstees.

Fig. 4-10 Ceiling tile or "planks" installed in suspended ceiling system.

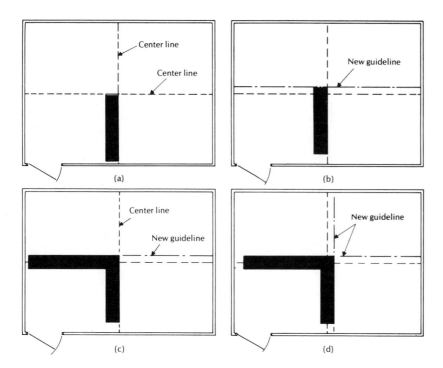

Fig. 4-11   Locating the center of a ceiling (or a floor) prior to installing tile. (Courtesy *The Home Repair Book,* J. G. Ferguson Publishing Co.)

electrical wiring, and open joists. We'll describe this system later in the book when we talk about basement remodeling.

Fig. 4–11 demonstrates the proper way to go about finding the center of a ceiling (or a floor) prior to installing the tiles. This method is important, because as a rule you'll want to install any short or narrow tile nearest the wall. In some cases, you might plan to create a border, installing a narrow row of tiles around the ceiling edges of the room.

Snap a chalkline. If the first row is to be narrower, cut the border tile to size. Most tiles are easily cut with a utility knife. Make sure of the measurement, and use a square to make sure your cut is true.

Place five daubs of adhesive on the tile, one in each corner and one in the center. Fit the tile into position in the starting corner. Make sure the stapling flange lines up on the chalkline. Then, holding the tile in position, staple through each flange. Staple the tile firmly so that the adhesive can take a tight hold. If there is excess adhesive, remove it at once, following the manufacturer's instructions.

To complete the ceiling, start along the edges of the two walls and then fill in between the bor-

ders with full–size tiles. The last step is to apply the molding.

If there is a lighting fixture in the ceiling, you can make an outline of the electrical outlet in the same way you made one to cut out a section of wallboard or a panel. Hold the tile up to the outlet. Cover a block of wood with a rag and, from the front of the tile, tap the tile against the outlet. This should leave an outline of the box. Drill four corners and then cut around the outline from the front of the tile using a sharp utility knife.

Instead of applying the tile directly to the ceiling, you can install wood furring strips to which the tile can be stapled. However, metal furring channels and crosstees, such as Armstrong's Intergrid^{TM} Furring Channel System, have become increasingly popular and offer several advantages. Because the tiles are laid or snapped into the channels, stapling is eliminated, making the installation easier. There is also a good chance you may be able to salvage the channels and crosstee if you need or want to change the ceiling design. Similarly, if you want to change the location of a lighting fixture, you may find making the change easier because the tiles can more easily be removed.

The initial steps in installing a metal furring channel and crosstee system are similar to those for direct-to-ceiling installations. Make your measurements carefully, whether you plan to install 12" x 12" tiles or 1" by 4" planks. Again, if a row of tile is to be narrower then the 12" size, plan to locate the last row against a wall or create a border on all four walls.

Begin with the channels, installing them perpendicular to the ceiling joists. Line one along the chalkline and nail it to the ceiling joists; then nail the other channels to the ceiling, making sure they are also lined up and square.

The next step is to nail a wall molding 3/4" below the channels around the perimeter of the room. From this stage on, installation should become even easier. Rest one of the 12" x 12" tiles or 1' x 4' panels on the wall molding and snap a crosstee into the channel. The crosstee slides into the slotted edges of the tile, locking it in place. Unlike direct-to-ceiling tile, these tiles are installed one row at a time across the room. Insert a wall spring at the end of the first row, between the tile and the wall. This spring keeps the tiles butted together. Continue installing tiles and crosstees until you reach the last row. The last row of tiles may need to be cut narrower and wall springs inserted to butt the rows of tiles firmly together across the width of the room as well as the length. The last tile is usually cut shorter on two sides, jiggled up through the hole and into position.

Were you planning to install a lighting fixture or two in the ceiling? If so, locate the opening for the fixture(s) in the same manner that you located it for the fixture in direct-to-ceiling tile. Remember that because this tile system is slightly lower (because of the channels, wall molding, and crosstees), you'll need a fixture having a base or covering that conceals the opening. Do *not* lower the outlet or move it from its sturdy location. Make sure wires are enclosed so they do *not* rub against channels. Again, if you need to work on the wiring, remember to shut off the power before you begin.

THE FLOOR

As mentioned earlier, you may have decided to install wood flooring, tile, or carpeting. Much depends on the purpose of the room. If the area becomes a recreation room, consider the occupants of the downstairs rooms. Nothing is more aggravating than trying to sleep while youngsters are rumpusing or teenagers rocking and rolling overhead.

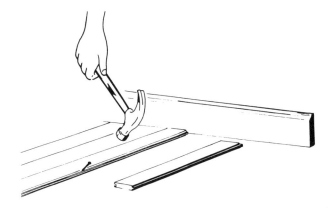

Fig. 4-12 Hammer nails at angle as shown, being careful not to damage tongues and grooves. (Courtesy *The Home Repair Book,* J. G. Ferguson Publishing Co.)

Wood flooring usually means tongue-and-groove boards, about 1/2" thick and varying in width from 3 1/2 to 7". Check the dimensions of the floor, length and width, including any alcoves or protruding sections such as closets to determine the quantity of flooring you'll need. The first board is laid against the wall after removing the tongue or groove with either a plane or a saw, or more often simply slipped under the wallboard or paneling. The board is fastened using 10d or 3"-long finish nails spaced 12" apart, hammered in at an angle through the groove and into the subflooring and joist below. See Fig. 4-12. The groove of the next board covers the nail head. Hammer the nails in neatly, using a punch if necessary so that you don't smash the tongue or groove. Broken and smashed pieces only make the next board more difficult to fit. Continue across the room until the entire floor is installed.

To finish a newly laid floor, only two sanding passes should be necessary: a first cut using medium grit (No. 1 1/2-40) sandpaper and a second cut using fine grit (No. 2/0-100) sandpaper. For a floor of any size, say 8' x 10', you'll need to rent a sander. Doing the job with a hand sander or by hand is a chore. Furthermore, you'll have difficulty in getting a smooth, uniform surface. When you rent a sander, practice using it on scrap wood flooring until you get the feel of it.

Take your time while sanding so that you do not gouge or scrape the wood. Try to blend each pass into the next. When sanding is completed, vacuum the floor thoroughly to remove the sawdust. Also vacuum walls and windowsills so that dust won't blow onto the floor when you apply the finish. Use a cloth dampened in alcohol to remove fine dust. Never use water. Water raises the wood grain requiring additional sanding.

To apply the finish, use a 4"–wide brush flowing the finish on smoothly and easily without overbrushing. Brush in the direction of the wood grain, doing three to five boards side by side at the same time.

You must sand the floor after the first coating because the first coat penetrates and tends to raise the grain. Hand sand the entire floor using fine sandpaper and vacuum or mop up all the dust. A second finish coating should be sufficient. Follow the manufacturer's instructions on the container as to sealers, types of brush or application, intervals between finishing coats, and other fine points.

Speaking of flooring, companies such as E. L. Bruce Co., Inc. make a variety of handsome parquets in blocks and squares that are installed by glueing, in the same manner that floor tile and carpeting are laid. You may wish to review some of the striking herringbone, basketweave, double-brick and other designs before making your final decision.

Laying Floor Tile

The correct way to lay floor tile is to start at the center of the room. By doing so, full-size tiles occupy most of the area with the tiles needing to be cut forming a border around the room. Some designs call for using a different tile color or design as the border.

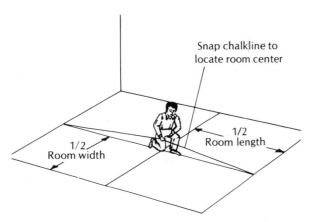

Snap chalkline to locate room center

1/2 Room length

1/2 Room width

Fig. 4-13 Snapping chalklines to line up tiles prior to installation.

First, measure half the distance of one wall and half the distance of the opposite wall. Pull a string tight from one midpoint to the other and snap a chalkline. Now repeat the process from the other two walls. Where the lines intersect is the center.

Measure from the center on all four lines to determine if the tiles will fit evenly in all four directions just as you did prior to installing ceiling tile. If there is a border of less than a half tile on one side, center a tile at the intersecting strings. Move the strings so they line up with the edges of the tile. Then check the intersecting lines with a square to make sure they are squared. See Fig. 4-13.

Follow the manufacturer's instructions for installing the floor tile as there are several different methods: applying mastic to the floor, applying adhesive to the back of the tile, and peel-and-stick.

Starting from the center of the room, lay several tiles along the chalklines making sure they are true and square. Fill in between the two rows with more tiles, working toward the walls. Cut the tile to be placed next to the walls to size, forming a border around the room. You may want to select a different tile for the border, harmonizing or contrasting designs and colors with those in the center of the room. If so, the time to make that decision is before you purchase the tile. Finish one quarter of the room before starting another section.

These directions have been simplified. Oftentimes there are corners jutting into the room or you must work around doorways, closets, built-in cabinets, radiators, etc. Take precise measurements and cut the tiles accurately. On the other hand, a smaller area may be easily tiled by starting from one corner and completing the entire area. Common sense and the dimensions of the room are your best guides.

Fitting around a pipe can be done in one of two ways. If the pipe reaches the subfloor and the connection will be made above floor level, outline the pupil and then cut the tile. To do so, (1) scribe the pipe circumference, (2) cut the hole in the tile, (3) extend the diameter of the hole across the tile to its edges, and (4) install the two separate but matching sections around the pipe.

Carpeting

Installing carpet tile is similar to laying floor tile, except that you should pay even more attention to

Peel-and-stick floor tiles make light work of installing a beautiful, durable floor. (Photo by the makers of Armstrong Flooring, Carpets, and Ceiling Systems)

the manufacturer's instructions. Some, if not most, types need to be acclimated in the room prior to installation. They must also be placed over clean floors, and if the floor is unfinished it should be sealed. Check the batch and numbers of the boxes in which you receive the material to make sure they are consecutive in case of variations in color or shade.

As with floor tile, you will need to snap chalklines to find the center of the room. Lay a tile where the lines intersect in the center of the room, make sure it is square and then press it down firmly. Then lay other tiles along the chalklines, filling in between the rows.

Wall-to-wall carpeting is stickier to handle in some ways, but certainly not impossible. Again, floor areas need to be clean and dry and the floor sealed. The floor should also be warm, about 60°–70° Fahrenheit. The carpeting should be unrolled a few days or more before installation so that it will stay flat and not curl or roll. Before purchasing carpeting, take precise measurements, but allow 3″ to 4″ extra on each side. This will be needed to carpet around outside corners and other projections.

Where the excess carpet climbs walls or doors, make relief cuts at the corners so these edges will begin to flatten. Then starting on one side, lift the carpet and fold it back a few inches. Use a piece of chalk to draw a line where floor and wall come together. Two lines should appear: one on the wall and one on the floor. These are trim lines. See Fig. 4-14.

Unfold the carpet and force it gently into the joint until it picks up the chalklines on the back or "downside." Make sure the lines are clear and unbroken, and that you know which is which, because next you'll cut along the line to trim the carpet. Cut with a sharp utility knife or razor, being careful to cut through only the carpeting you want to cut, and allow the carpet to fall into position so that the edges touch the wall or molding.

Trimming around obstacles such as pipes is performed by cutting toward the obstacle. *Do it gradually*—making several relief cuts rather than one slash.

To complete the installation you will need to tape the edge of the carpet to the floor wherever there is a door or where the carpet ends on open flooring. Make a light pencil mark along the carpet edge. Fold back the carpet. Apply double-faced carpet tape along the line, placing the tape on the

Fig. 4-14 Making a relief cut in carpeting to fit it against a corner.

side where the carpet is being installed. Press the tape down firmly and then press the carpet edge on the exposed tape. After tape and carpet are in proper position, press down by walking over the edge or use a rolling pin.

DOORS/WINDOWS

You may or may not have decided to install a door in the upstairs room. Much depends on the size of the room and the uses you have in mind.

Good, sturdy preassembled doors and frames are readily available. The kit or package you buy will probably come from stock rather than being the unit you examined on the dealer's floor. After you bring it home check the condition of the wood, and make sure the dimensions are correct. Stand the unit up and make sure it is square.

Preassembled units are easy to install. They involve fitting the frame in the doorway, fastening the frame to header and jack studs, and installing hinges, knob, lock, and strike plate.

On the other hand, you may decide not to buy a package and to install the door yourself. Take the measurements, remembering that a 1/8″ clearance is the minimum necessary all around to assure a free swing. To install the door you will need to

1. Trim the door to height, removing any stiles or horns (protruding pieces of wood sometimes left on unfinished wood). Use a jack or smoothing plane, working from the outside edge toward the center to avoid splintering.

2. Place door in opening *upside down*.

3. Keep hinge side tight against jamb.

4. Raise door 1/4″ using shims.

5. Mark door across top (actually the bottom) where it fits against the top plate.

6. Cut to height.

7. Place door in opening in correct position and raise 1/8".

8. Have another person draw a line along the lock side, from the other side of the door.

9. Trim to size. The fit should be sufficiently close (on all sides) so that trimming is done with a plane.

10. Bevel lock side of door to approximately 3° angle.

11. Hinges are usually placed 7" from top of door and 9" from bottom. Mortises for hinges must be of uniform depth to accommodate the hinges and ensure free swinging.

12. If door does not swing smoothly, further planing and sanding may be necessary. Shims may also need to be inserted under door sill and between studs and jambs.

13. Unfinished doors should be primed before painting.

14. Install knob, lock, and strike plate.

The procedure for installing a window or windows in an upstairs room is almost identical to that for installing a roof window. Instead of cutting through roof shingles, however, you will be cutting through siding or wall shingles. You will want to check the condition of the studs, sheathing, and siding or shingles before making the installation. You should also check with your building inspector as to local codes including safety glass regulations.

There are all types of preassembled window kits: gliding, double–hung, casement, awning, picture, bay, and bow windows. Choose the style that best blends into the architecture of your home. Also consider double–pane types for energy savings. If you live in a northern part of the country, install the window(s) facing south so that you obtain the warmth of the sun in winter.

In general, installing a window is not difficult provided you make the cut the proper size and frame the opening correctly. Check level, plumb, and square. Insulate between jambs and studs. Check the installation and operation of the window before applying the interior trim.

More details on installing windows are provided in Chapter 6, where installing windows in a converted garage or carport is described.

PAPERING

Wallpapering is a skill requiring patience. Some folks have it, others don't. Some people consider adhesive–backed wallpapers the biggest boon to man since the wheel.

The wall being covered should be clean, smooth, and dry. Protruding nails need to be countersunk. Electric switch and outlet covers should be removed. Unlike paneling, wallpaper is applied over the opening and the outline slit from the finished side. The fixture covers will conceal ragged edges.

Start by using a plumbline to draw a chalkline from ceiling to floor. Attach line to ceiling and let it drop. Snap the line and make sure top and bottom are square.

Measure the first strip of paper according to the height of the wall. Allow a few extra inches at the bottom. Do not apply the first strip at a corner. Start at least 1" to either side because the corner strip must be folded into the corner.

The walls must be sized if paste is used. Apply paste to back of paper wetting the paper thoroughly. Fold the strip in half. Apply the top half to top portion of the wall while letting the bottom fold drop. Working quickly before the paste hardens, move the strip into position pressing it lightly against the wall. Sponge each strip to smooth it and remove excess paste. Avoid bulges or wrinkles. Keeping the paper wet permits you to make minor adjustments if the strip isn't quite straight. Flatten the seams between two strips with a roller.

Papering around door and window frames is performed by scribing, carefully measuring the sections to be cut, in the same manner as for paneling.

PAINTING

Painting interior walls and molding is one of the most common chores or pleasures. Homeowners have painted the walls of their residences since the days of Cro–Magnon man and perhaps earlier. Instructions for painting are printed on every can of paint and in dozens if not hundreds of booklets. Still, a few words of advice may be useful to the inexperienced:

1. Flat paints are used primarily on wide surfaces for a no–glare finish. Semi– and high–gloss paints are better for surfaces that are used and abused: doors, molding.

Bright printed fabrics give a finished look to this room. Walls and ceiling are simply rough painted boards. Designed by Shirley Regendahl. (Courtesy Waverly Fabrics)

Wall treatments for this basement room include painted board, paneling and wallpaper to match the fabric of the chair. Room design by Barbara Egner. (Courtesy Waverly Fabrics)

Wallcovering Estimating Chart *

Distance Around Room in Feet	Single Rolls for Wall Areas Height of Ceiling			Number Yards For Borders	Single Rolls For Ceilings
	8 Feet	9 Feet	10 Feet		
28	8	8	10	11	2
30	8	8	10	11	2
32	8	10	10	12	2
34	10	10	12	13	4
36	10	10	12	13	4
38	10	12	12	14	4
40	10	12	12	15	4
42	12	12	14	15	4
44	12	12	14	16	4
46	12	14	14	17	6
48	14	14	16	17	6
50	14	14	16	18	6
52	14	14	16	19	6
54	14	16	18	19	6
56	14	16	18	20	8
58	16	16	18	21	8
60	16	18	20	21	8
62	16	18	20	22	8
64	16	18	20	23	8
66	18	20	22	23	10
68	18	20	22	24	10
70	18	20	22	25	10
72	18	20	22	25	12
74	20	22	22	26	12
76	20	22	24	27	12
78	20	22	24	27	14
80	20	22	26	28	14
82	22	24	26	29	14
84	22	24	26	30	16
86	22	24	26	30	16
88	24	26	28	31	16[
90	24	26	28	32	18

* Deduct one single roll for every two average-size doors or windows.

Use this table to estimate number of rolls of wallpaper needed to cover walls in a single room or rooms. (Courtesy *The Home Repair Book*, J. G. Ferguson Publishing Co.)

2. Oil–base paints may have more lasting qualities but latex–base paints make cleaning up easier.

3. Hairline cracks can be filled with paint but anything larger will require spackling and sanding. Remember to remove all sawdust.

4. Bare, unsealed, previously unpainted surfaces can sometimes be painted without a primer, but they will never look as good as they should. Do the job right; the additional cost and effort are worth the trouble.

5. Using dropcloths is neater and quicker than removing drips and spots.

6. Removing switchplates and outlet covers is easier than painting around them. Removing or painting around doorknobs and hinges takes approximately the same time. Paint before you install them.

7. Pad–type applicators and edgers work very well especially if you've never learned to wield a brush without rebrushing and rebrushing.

8. Use a roller with 4'–long handle extension to paint ceilings. Doing so provides a better perspective and is less tiring than climbing up and down a stepladder.

9. Masking tape is a poor substitute for a steady hand when painting those long dividing lines between walls and ceilings.

10. Figure on applying two coats of paint over most wide areas. A one–coat job requires professional skill.

11. Paint the ceiling first.

5

BEAUTIFYING
THE BASEMENT

Now that your attic has become an upstairs room, your attention may turn downward to the basement with all its space and possibilites, including everything moved from the attic to the basement. What to do with it all? One thought is a yard sale, or a trip to one of the many charitable organizations that can make good use of things that are no longer needed.

Basement areas offer all sorts of interesting ideas: a recreation room, bedroom, study, music or hobby room, or several rooms such as a sports corner, darkroom, and perhaps others.

Much of the information presented in this book about remodeling the attic is also applicable to basement areas. A partition is raised in much the same way on either floor. Paneling is similar. So are tiling and carpeting. Rather than repeat information you already know, this chapter provides information you need to renovate a basement. First is the subject of waterproofing.

WATERPROOFING

There is no point in finishing a basement if there is a major water or seepage problem. Water will cause damage like staining and mildew and eventual deterioration.

The source of a water problem is usually outside the house (although more than one farmhouse was intentionally built over a spring!) and is due to poor drainage. Check the gutters and downspouts. Downspouts should carry the water at least ten feet away from the house to drywells, drainage basins, or community sewer or waste–water lines. Poor soil grading is another source of water prob-

lems. Such problems should be corrected whether or not you renovate the basement because they can affect the value of your home.

Water or seepage problems that are not too serious can often be corrected by sealing cracked or porous walls. This is accomplished by applying basement waterproofing compounds to the inside basement walls.

First make sure the walls are clean. Give them a good vacuuming. Scrape off loose material with a wire brush. Widen large cracks by first undercutting them and then shaping them into V's, widening each crack at the surface or opening and narrowing it as it deepens, then fill with cement or a waterproofing compound. If your basement has cinder block walls, check for loose mortar between the blocks and repair.

There are a number of waterproofing compounds that can be applied on cinder block or concrete using a rough brush. Do not rely on ordinary paints; they don't have sufficient strength to resist seepage. Compounds for waterproofing basement are generally heavy, of a creamy consistency, and should be brushed on liberally. Apply an epoxy sealer where the basement walls meet the floor, overlapping the two by at least three or four inches.

Inasmuch as you will be enclosing the cinder block or concrete walls and covering the floor, you don't need to be too fussy about your paint job. In some places applying more than one coating may be necessary. This is unfortunate but essential.

One other point: do the waterproofing job long before you remodel the basement. Long enough so that you can be sure it is effective. Don't, for example, waterproof the basement

Your basement workshop beside an outside doorway you've installed yourself. (Courtesy The Bilco Company)

A basement is a "catch-all" until someone makes it into a rumpus room or recreation area.

during a dry spell and then remodel. A rainy season could show that you didn't do a very good job.

ROUGHING IN THE BASEMENT

Roughing in the basement is similar to roughing in the attic. But there are obvious differences. For one, you will need to nail bottom plates and perhaps studs or uprights to masonry, either cinder block or concrete. You will also want to conceal objects such as the furnace, hot water tank, washing machine and dryer, and certainly overhead piping and wiring. You may, more logically, want to install a bathroom downstairs rather than upstairs. And perhaps you will find that a doorway directly to the outdoors is not only a convenience but a necessity.

To make partitions separating one room or area from another, you can fasten the 2 x 4 floor plate by hammering it in with hardened masonry stell nails. Drive the nails through the wood first and then into the concrete. Use 10-20d (3-4" long) nails. Hit them squarely, otherwise they may bend. Also, stagger the row of nails for greater holding power.

Expansion-type anchors and shields which hold screws and lagging bolts are also used. With an adjustable- or variable-speed electric drill, drill a hole in the masonry using a carbide-tipped drill bit. Always drive the bit slowly, under 400 rpm, and hold the drill firmly so that the bit does not slip or wiggle. Drill the hole the approximate width and distance and then insert the anchor or shield until it is flush with the wall or floor. Drill through

Part of the basement becomes a "sports arena" after you've made your point. (Photo by the makers of Armstrong Flooring, Carpets, and Ceiling Systems)

the wood being fastened and then insert the bolt or screw through the wood and into the anchor or shield. The action of the screw or bolt will expand the shield in the wall and should provide a tight, secure fastening.

Stud drivers are also available for driving in fasteners and are considerably faster and easier to use if your project is extensive. They can often be rented if you can't borrow one from a contractor friend.

Nailing a 2 x 4 to the basement ceiling joists is usually no problem. Just be careful not to drive the nail through wiring or piping or to hit either when you raise the hammer to strike.

Incidentally, this is a good time to install steel jack posts or lollycolumns if your basement

Would you believe there are overhead pipes and ducts, and a steel post, concealed in this downstairs room? (Photo by the makers of Armstrong Flooring, Carpets, and Ceiling Systems)

Installing foam insulation in basement for extra comfort. (Courtesy W. R. Grace & Co., Construction Products Division)

Paneling over lightweight foam panel insulation adds comfort winter and summer to a basement room. (Courtesy W. R. Grace & Co., Construction Products Division)

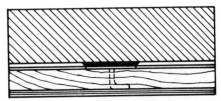

On masonry—use nail anchors or adhesive anchors.

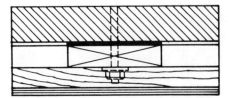

On masonry—bolt anchors may be used for attaching 1" x 3" sub-furring to wall then attach 1" x 2" furring to 1" x 3" as if to studs.

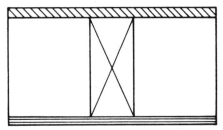

On masonry—2" x 3" framing wedged to ceiling and floor. (Alternate treatment—lay framing flat against wall.)

Fig. 5-1 Fasteners used in attaching furring to masonry walls. (Courtesy Georgia-Pacific Corporation)

doesn't have them, or if there are signs of the floor above beginning to sag. Check the level of the basement girders. If there are signs of sagging, purchase two or more telescoping jack posts and insert them under the sagging girder or beam. They must be jacked up very slowly—beginning with exerting the slightest pressure and then turned about one-half turn a week for several months.

You should also consider insulating the basement, especially the portion above ground. Inexpensive insulating boards or panels are now available that offer R–2 or R–3 values.

Installing these foam boards or panels is an easy job, as shown in photographs on page 79. All you need to do is nail furring strips the thickness (1

1/2"–2") of the panels to the basement walls, making sure the furring strips and panels are flush and square. Figure 5–1 shows the different types of fasteners used in attaching furring to masonry. The foam panels are easily cut using either a hand or power saw.

You can also insulate with 3 1/2"– or 4"–thick batts or blankets to provide more insulation. To do this, you will need to erect a partition using a 2 x 4 top plate that is fastened to the ceiling joists in order to allow space for the insulation. (Driving nails or inserting bolts through the 4" side of a 2 x 4 into a masonry wall is not recommended.)

The partition should be installed 4"-5" from the wall which will reduce the basement perimeter slightly, but increase the comfort of the room. The foil side of the insulation must face the living area. Insulate behind pipes especially because they will now be isolated from the warmth of the basement room. (Note: Basement insulation of this type may not be advisable in areas where there are extreme freeze–thaw conditions. So, check locally.)

A suspended ceiling should conceal most of the ducts, pipes, and cables installed in the exposed basement ceiling. However, there may be places where you need to "lower the ceiling." The easiest way is to nail 2 x 2's or 2 x 3's ("hangers") vertically from the joists. Make sure they are square and level. Join the hangers opposite each other by nailing crosspieces of the same size between them. Then nail 1 x 3's to frame the hanger on the exposed sides. This may involve framing the hanger on one, two, or three sides depending on the object and the location of the walls. The hangers can then be enclosed with wallboard, paneling, or other material you have selected.

Similar steps are involved in enclosing a furnace. You will need a 2 x 4 floor or bottom plate and a top plate. You will also need to erect 2 x 4 uprights or studs, figuring 16" on center or as needed to frame the walls. However, a note of caution. Don't enclose the furnace too tightly. In addition to fire–safety precautions, the furnace needs air to breathe. It also needs to let its heat radiate outward. At least one side must be left open for maintenance.

The same factors apply to ductwork and piping. If you enclose them tightly, you will send more heat upstairs, but lose heat in the basement. Allow 3-4' around the furnace and 3-4" around ductwork and piping. A material to consider for these applications is pegboard, which allows

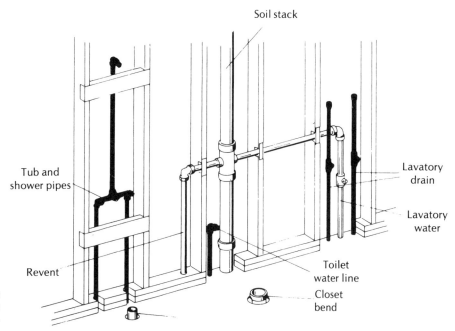

Fig. 5-2 Basic bathroom plumbing arrangement. (Courtesy *The Home Repair Book,* J. G. Ferguson Publishing Co.)

areas facing the room can be painted and decoample flow of air. At the same time, the pegboard rated to blend with the overall decor.

ELECTRICAL WIRING

Pages 39–46 provided information about extending electrical wiring, but pointed out the importance of checking local building code regulations and the condition of wiring in your home. Because of the proximity of the fuse box or circuit breaker, there is greater temptation to make basement connections directly. A word of advice: *don't* unless you are a licensed electrician, because you will most likely be working with 210–220 volts.

You may wish to move some wires and cables out of the way of partitions and paneling. This can be done by taking the following steps: (1) SHUT OFF THE POWER, (2) disconnect the cable, (3) drill through the necessary ceiling joists, (4) reconnect the cable, (5) check your work, and (6) restore the power. Cables can also be fastened to overhead boards.

PLUMBING FIXTURES

A downstairs bathroom is frequently desirable and often a necessity. Installing one may be less costly than installing an upstairs bathroom because of

the proximity to water supply and drainage lines.

Here again, you will need to check local building code regulations and contact a plumber. This is necessary because although connecting to the incoming water supply doesn't present problems, the outgoing waste and water will unless properly removed through the drainage pipes. Sinks and toilet installations are usually made more easily because they are sufficiently elevated for proper drainage through the outgoing lines.

A bathtub, bath–shower combination, or stall shower will need to be located above the level of the drainage pipe. This in turn may mean breaking through the basement floor and wall to the outdoor lines to establish a lower connecting point, or perhaps the unit can be elevated in order to assure drainage.

But let's assume your friendly building inspector and/or plumber has agreed to let you make the connections, enabling you to save additional labor costs. You know the kind of instructions: "O.K. There's the hot and there's the cold. And that's where the water goes out."

Following his instructions, and with additional information, you should be able to connect the three bathroom fixtures to the proper piping. Fig. 5–2 shows the roughed–in plumbing for the vanity or sink, toilet, and tub and shower pipes. Fig. 5–3 shows how this basic piping actually ties into the three fixtures.

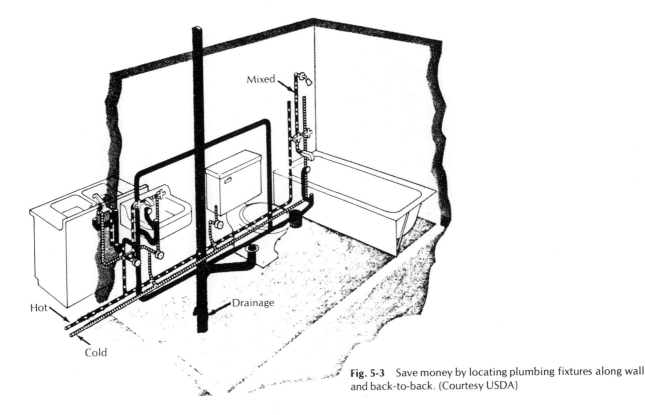

Mixed

Hot

Cold

Drainage

Fig. 5-3   Save money by locating plumbing fixtures along wall and back-to-back. (Courtesy USDA)

A few other tips about plumbing. You can save considerable time and money by locating fixtures back-to-back against a wall—for example, locating a bathroom sink on the other side of the wall from a downstairs sink, as shown in Fig. 5-3, or a washtub. Locating all of the fixtures on the same wall will also minimize piping costs. Installing hot-water fixtures near the hot-water heater will help shorten piping runs and also reduce the loss of heat in transmission from the heater to the fixture.

Check to make sure there are no leaks in the drainage or outgoing systems, and also that there are no connections between the water supply and drainage systems. (Plumbers, too, are sometimes absentminded!) And make sure there is no back-up from any fixture into the water-supply system. If a new vent stack is installed, make sure that it rises sufficiently high above the roof so that it cannot be blocked by snow.

Today's cabinet types of vanities and tankless toilets eliminate the need to fasten these fixtures to walls, but if you do install a wall fixture, make sure that it is properly supported. Fig. 5-4 shows the wood blocking behind a wall-mounted sink.

Use 2 x 4's nailed level and square between the uprights.

Bathroom partitions, walls, and ceilings are installed before tiling. However, while speaking of plumbing and these fixtures is a good time to provide tiling instructions. Preassembled shower stalls are quite easy to install and instructions are provided by the manufacturer. So let's consider the matter of tiling a newly installed bath–shower combination.

Installing a number of separate tiles is no longer necessary. Manufacturers such as American Olean offer pregrouted glazed ceramic tile sheets with as many as 16 tiles per sheet. A typical sheet covers a 2 square foot area or larger. These tile sheets can be installed over wallboard, masonry, plywood, or plaster and other materials. Internal corner strips are also available and are a good idea to make sure water being splashed and sprayed remains totally in the enclosure.

Tile above a set-in bathtub to a height of 56″ to 80″. Tile height above the base of a shower should be from 72″ to 92″.

Holes for fixtures should be predrilled from the back of the tile sheet. Again, outline the circum-

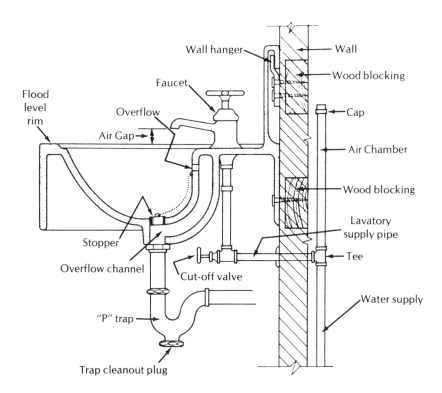

Wall hanger

Faucet

Wall

Wood blocking

Flood level rim

Overflow

Air Gap

Cap

Air Chamber

Stopper

Wood blocking

Overflow channel

Lavatory supply pipe

Cut-off valve

Tee

"P" trap

Water supply

Trap cleanout plug

Fig. 5-4 Support wall-mounted fixtures with 2 x 4" blocking between uprights. (Courtesy USDA)

Installing bathroom tile with easy-to-use sections against roughened adhesive applied to wall. (Courtesy American Olean Tile Co.)

Cornerpieces are a good investment against spraying water when installing a downstairs bath or shower. (Courtesy American Olean Tile Co.)

Grouting is necessary only between panels' sides and ends. Use an ordinary caulking gun. (Courtesy American Olean Tile Co.)

ference of the hole by holding the panel against the pipe opening and tapping gently until you make an indented outline.

Grouting is necessary only between the sheets, along corner strips, and where the tile joins other surfaces. You will, however, need to apply a mortar backing to the wall, which can be a conventional mortar, dry-set mortar, or organic adhesive. This backing should be applied either in a rough circular manner or in a criss-cross pattern to ensure good adhesion. (Follow manufacturer's instructions.) A standard caulking gun can be used to grout between the sheets. Grouting air guns are also used.

FINISHING THE BASEMENT

Once the basement is roughed in—partitions erected, insulation in place, plumbing and electrical fixtures and outlets installed—much of the remaining work is similar to that in renovating the attic. Wallboard or gypsumboard is installed in the

same manner, so is paneling and perhaps even the ceiling.

Basement ceilings, as a rule, are not as easy to cover. There are projections and protuberances—electrical cables and piping—that you would like to conceal but cannot hide under direct-to-ceiling tiles or planks. You may not want to go to the expense and labor of moving the pipes. At the same time, you would like to have the ceiling flush from one end of the room to the other.

Suspended ceilings differ from other types in using "hangers" which can be installed to lower the ceiling to almost any height you desire. These hangers are inserted through screw eyes into the joists and then bent at the bottom to accommodate runners (channels) and crosstees.

To install a suspended ceiling:

1. Determine the distance you need to lower the ceiling.
2. Make your measurements at the lowest point.
3. Nail wall molding around the perimeter of the room.
4. Mark off the measurements to install the screw eyes in the ceiling joists. (The number of screw eyes and their locations will depend on the size of the tiles (2' x 2') or panels (2' x 4') and the channels and crosstees.)
5. Install the screw eyes. Start them in with a light blow from a hammer if necessary and then twist them in with a stick or screwdriver.
6. Install the hanger wires, twisting them at the top and then bending them to a 90° angle using a pair of pliers. (See Fig. 5–5.)
7. Suspend the main runners in rows perpendicular to the joist direction. (Built-in splices, end tabs, and precut holes are built into Armstrong Lay-in Panel Suspension Systems if you need to splice two or more sections together.)
8. Snap the crosstees into the main runners.
9. Drop the ceiling panels into the grid, setting each on the flanges of both the runners and crosstees as shown in Fig. 5–6.
10. If one row needs to be narrower, locate it along one wall or establish a border around the perimeter as described in installing other types of ceilings.

Speaking of ceilings, you may want to install the simulated beams so popular today under a wallboard ceiling. These beams simulate the

How to turn a corner of the basement into a comfortable entertainment alcove. A Barbara A. Egner room design. (Courtesy Waverly Fabrics)

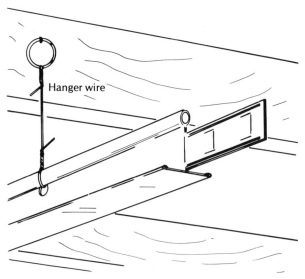

Fig. 5-5 Bend the hanger wires to a 90° angle, using a pair of pliers.

Fig. 5-6 Set the ceiling panel into the grid flanges on runners and crosstees.

appearance of weathered beams in eighteeth-century colonial houses or the Ponderosa Ranch. Made of lightweight polyurethane foam, they can be cut with a knife and are easy to handle. They also resist warping, termites, rotting, and fungus.

The first step (as always) is to measure the ceiling distances. Sketch the pattern or design you intend to create: length of room, width of room, and intersections. (With the right design, you can even play tic-tac-toe on the ceiling!)

Stretch chalklines across the ceiling and snap them. Or use a tape measure to locate exactly where the beams should be installed.

Make sure the ceiling is dry and clean. If you have already given the ceiling a high-gloss finish painting, sand the area where the beams are to be installed in order to provide good adhesion.

Cut beams to length using a miter. Installation is usually a two-person task, one on each end of the beam. When ready to install the beam, apply adhesive on the side of the beam to contact the ceiling. Press into place. Support the beam by bracing it with 2 x 4's cut approximately the distance from the floor to the ceiling. But protect the beam finish by covering the ends of the 2 x 4's with pads or rags.

Use two or three supports per 10' of beam length to prevent sagging or wobbling. If you are not sure the beam is perfectly straight, check the angles at both sides of the room with a square in those few minutes before the adhesive begins to set.

Two beams can be butted as needed. Apply adhesive on the butting ends and press the ends firmly together while holding them against the ceiling. Follow the manufacturer's instructions concerning the length of time the beams should be braced.

A BASEMENT DOORWAY

Your downstairs recreation or family room may lack one convenience: easy access and egress. Doors and stairs to the basement typically open from a kitchen, hall, or other room. An outside door would help eliminate traffic through the kitchen and also provide an easy means of going outdoors to a swimming pool, patio, or garden.

First, you'll need to locate the new entrance for the doorway (which used to be called a "bulkhead"). Choose a place where it will not interfere with partitions, utility lines, or piping, and away from areas that are potentially hazardous such as the furnace, fireplace, or garage.

You'll also need to consider the grading and slope of the land around the house. If the land slopes toward the location where you would like to install the door you should choose another location. Otherwise, the doorwell may collect rain and snow unless properly drained and protected.

When you have selected the location, measure the height of the grade (or yard or land) above your basement floor. Then using the table on page 87, determine how much soil you will need to excavate for the outside stairway. The figure is calculated by measuring the height of the grade

The difference between a closed-in downstairs room and a light, bright rec room is sometimes only a doorway. (Courtesy The Bilco Company)

HEIGHT OF GRADE ABOVE FINISHED BASEMENT FLOOR WILL BE:	BUILD AREAWAY TO THESE (INSIDE) DIMENSIONS:			USE THIS BILCO DOOR AND EXTENSION		USE THESE BILCO STAIR STRINGERS & EXTENSIONS (SIZE E EXTENSION HAS 3-TREAD RUN)	STRINGER UNIT HAS 8¼" RISE, 8⅜" RUN AND 1⅛" NOSING	
	H*	L	W	Door Size	Extension Size		Treads in Areaway	Run+ in Areaway
2' 0" to 2' 7"‡	2' 9"	3' 4"	3' 8"	SL	None	(Not Available)	3	2' 2¼"
2' 8" to 3' 3"	3' 5¼"	3' 4"	3' 8"	SL	None	SL	4	2' 10⅝"
4' 0" to 4' 7"‡‡	4' 9¾"	4' 6"	3' 4"	O	None	O	6	4' 3⅜"
4' 8" to 5' 4"‡‡	5' 6"	5' 0"	3' 8"	B	None	B	7	4' 11¾"
5' 5" to 6' 0"	6' 2¼"	5' 8"	4' 0"	C	None	C	8	5' 8⅛"
6' 1" to 6' 8"	6' 10½"	6' 8"	4' 0"	C	12"	O + E	9	6' 4½"
6' 9" to 7' 4"	7' 6¾"	7' 2"	4' 0"	C	18"	B + E	10	7' 0⅞"
7' 5" to 8' 1"	8' 3"	7' 9"	4' 0"	C	24"	C + E	11	7' 9¼"

*Above Finished Basement Floor   ‡Maximum House Wall 7' 1"   ‡‡Maximum House Wall 7' 4"   +Run plus 1⅛" Nosing on Bottom Tread

above your finished basement floor. If the height is 2′ to 2′7″, you'll need to excavate an area 2′9″ deep x 3′4″ long x 3′8″ wide.

If the doorway needs to be located farther below ground, a more extensive excavating job will be needed to accommodate the descending stairs. For example: if the height of the grade is 7′5″ to 8′1″, you will need to excavate an area that is 8′3″ deep, 7′9″ long, and 4′ wide. Allow an additional 1′ for waterproofing and space for footing. Then excavate to about 4″ below the footing of the foundation.

To open the basement wall you will first need to outline the area to break through. A cinder block wall can be broken through in three or four hours with a special power drill, available from rental shops or masonry supply houses.

If the wall is poured concrete, you will need to borrow or rent an electric hammer with chisel attachment. If it is one of those mammoth concrete and stone foundations that contractors built until recent years, you will definitely need to hire a special contractor.

Use a sledge hammer to knock out the wall, working from inside out to make removing blocks, mortar, and concrete cleaner and easier.

Take the precaution of closing the wall opening with plastic sheeting if you do not complete the job by nightfall. Similarly, if you must leave the excavation unattended or overnight, take the precaution of building a temporary fence around it to minimize the risk of people or animals falling into the hole.

The materials you will need to make the doorway include concrete, masonry block, mortar cement, sand, drainage tile, waterproofing compound, treads, door, caulking, and paint. Because of the variations in soil, water table, and climate conditions, you must check carefully with the building inspector and local professionals to determine the proper proportions of concrete and mortar. What is appropriate in the rocky soil and rainy climate of New England is not likely to be correct in dry, sandy areas or under tropical conditions.

First lay out the concrete footing as a base. Follow the manufacturer's directions including those for building forms. The concrete will need to set before laying the blocks for the walls. When the concrete has set, the first row of cinder blocks can be laid. Check your measurements carefully from one corner to the next, making sure the lines are straight and the corners square. Use a tightly stretched string as a chalkline.

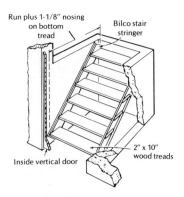

Fig. 5-7 Detail for an outside doorway to the downstairs room. (Courtesy The Bilco Company)

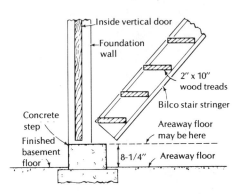

Fig. 5-8 Horizontal view of a doorway installation to a downstairs room. (Courtesy The Bilco Company)

You will then need to mix and lay a bed of mortar (check with local professionals as to composition, mixing, setting, etc.), butting the cinderblocks against each other and "buttering" each one on the ends. Check to make sure they are level and straight, using a level and a straightedge to align them.

Build up the corners first, a level or two higher than the row you will lay next. Lay a row at a time, mortaring the tops of the blocks below. As each few blocks are laid, double-check alignment and level. When all the blocks are laid, you will need to cap the wall with concrete. Build wood forms to bring the top to the correct level. See Fig. 5–7.

Basement door units are available that permit you to attach a sturdy metal door in the wall. This is installed before pouring concrete for the cap. Available in knocked-down kits, these units should contain detailed instructions for installation.

After the door is installed, the areaway must be poured, troweled, and allowed to set. If the doorway is properly installed, provisions for drainage should not be necessary. In case of doubt or as a long-term precautionary measure, you may wish to provide for drainage, which should be done after the excavation but before erecting the masonry wall. This will involve installing a drain and laying drainpipe connected to a dry well.

Stairs are also available in kits including stringers (into which the stairs or treads are set), the treads and masonry fasteners. See Figure 5–8.

The now–inside vertical door should be relatively easy to install, using prefabricated assembled kits that include door and frame. You may need to build a primary door frame first using lumber that is the same width as the width of the foundation. Any rough or jagged pieces of masonry will need to be smoothed so that the wood fits snugly. You may also need to reduce the width of the foundation to conform to the size of the door. This is accomplished by using lumber of smaller and smaller widths, i.e., 2 x 8's, 2 x 6's, 2 x 4's, and half–rounds in order to provide a finished appearance. Mortar cracks should be filled in and spaces and shims used to ensure the alignment and squareness of the frame.

New concrete usually takes several weeks to dry, so the areaway may (and probably will) be damp for some time. You can alleviate this condition by leaving the door open in good weather to dissipate the moisture. Within a month or two, the condition should correct itself and the doorway area remain dry.

More detailed information on this subject is available in the booklet, "Ideas for a Living Basement" offered by The Bilco Co., Dept. BC, New Haven, Conn. 06505. For a copy, enclose 25¢ for handling and postage.

6

CONVERTING
CARPORTS/GARAGES

Attic and basement renovations differ, and carport or garage remodeling differs from them both. The overhead door of the garage must be removed and replaced with sheathing and siding or shingles, and walls must be built for the carport on one, two, and perhaps three sides. If the carport has no floor, a solid foundation and floor must be provided.

But much of the work is similar to what you have already performed: partitioning, paneling, installing ceilings, etc. The extension of wiring (if you are permitted to do the work yourself) is almost identical to the wiring done in other areas. There's a likelihood you may want to add plumbing facilities, but it is not very probable. On the other hand, provisions will need to be made for heating if you live in a cool climate.

CONVERTING THE GARAGE

If you already have a closed-in garage, you'll need to remove the overhead door(s) and the fixtures and trim. You will also need to continue the foundation through the area that was formerly door-space, as well as sheath and side the open area.

A task to which you may need to give immediate attention is the floor. Installing wood, tile or carpeting over an oily, greasy garage floor is a mistake you will pay for sooner or later. Why bother to track through the stuff now?

First, scrape off as much of the oil and grease as you can with a putty knife or scraper. Pour a driveway cleaner over the surface. Let the cleaner dissolve and soften the oil and grease, and work into the surface pores. Thoroughly scrub the area

with a long-handled brush or broom. Mop up the dirty sludge and wash the emulsion away. Then rinse the entire area with clean water and let it dry.

Many strong cleaning compounds can cause irritations and rashes to sensitive skin even through clothing. Be careful handling them. If contact is made with hands, feet, etc. immediately wash the affected area. Note the caution notice on the container and follow directions for applying the product and in case contact is made.

CONVERTING THE CARPORT

Rather than describe the steps involved in converting a garage, let's start from scratch—and assume you have a carport consisting of plastic roof panels supported by a few uprights set in concrete. Only the side to the house is a wall.

You'll need to check your local building code. Although you may get away without a permit for some of the inside work, enclosing a carport is similar to making a brand-new addition and the construction is open for all to see.

First, you'll need to figure out the measurements. Will the area of the new room be the same area as the carport? Or do you plan to make it larger?

To make the measurements, mark the length desired on the side of the house. Drive in stakes at both ends and hammer a nail into the top of each stake. Set two more stakes out to establish the width. Then figure 90° angles from the first two stakes, using a 4' x 8' sheet of plywood to square up the corners. Stretch strong builder's string between the stakes. The distances of the diago-

This could have been your unfinished garage, now being converted into an extra room.

nals, or the hypotenuses of the triangles, which you have established from the first and second stakes should be equal and form the square or rectangular room shape you plan. See Fig. 6–1.

Unless you plan to construct a basement under the new room, a concrete slab is the simplest method of establishing a foundation. In this way, the footing, foundation and slab are poured in one massive slab.

However, in northern climates, the foundation and slab are poured separately. A sheet of polyethylene, which forms a vapor barrier, is placed between the foundation and slab. A rigid foam insulation panel should also be installed to protect the room from cold coming up from the ground as shown in the technical drawing, Fig. 6–2.

Pouring concrete for a foundation is a major job for a husband–and–wife team because it means pouring 200 sq. ft. or more of concrete, at least 4″ thick, and reinforcing it with rods or wire mesh in one operation.

The concrete will first need a bed—6″ to 12″ deep of free-draining sand, crushed stone, gravel, and cinders—which must be tamped down until it is compact. Forms of plywood must be built before the concrete is poured.

A few words about concrete. It has many compositions. Portland cement, sand, gravel (or crushed stone), and clean water make up the basic compositions. However, the ingredients, quantities, mixing and application are critical factors—as in baking a cake—and all of them must be precise.

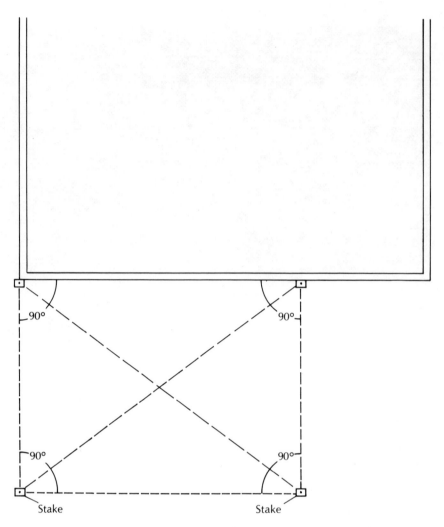

90°   90°

90°   90°

Stake   Stake

Fig. 6-1 How to establish the measurements to add a room to your home.

Too little water will make the concrete difficult if not impossible to work with. Too much water will make the concrete easier to use but can produce a weak mixture which will be deleterious in the long run if not earlier.

You can buy cement, sand, gravel, and add water to make your own mixture, and then rent a portable mixer. However, the foundation or slab should be poured at one time otherwise you will have seams between the sections that will only create later problems. The best advice is to engage a reliable local contractor who can pour the mixed ingredients from his truck. (If this is your first contact with contractors, remember that most are honest and hard working. They are more interested in their reputations and repeat business than mak-

ing a fast buck, and can be extremely helpful to you in avoiding problems and even disasters.)

Once the concrete is poured, it will need to be leveled. It can be spread with the back of a rake, filling in holes and leveling high points.

Concrete must also be "screeded" using a length of 2 x 4 set on the edges of the forms. Move the 2 x 4 along the forms in a sawing motion. Level the surface and then remove the excess. A "float" is also used to raise some of the fine particles in the mixture and to settle larger pieces of aggregate. The concrete should not be allowed to dry immediately; damp-dried concrete is stronger than concrete that is allowed to sit unattended. Cover the slab with straw and fine spray it with water two or three times a day for a week. If the

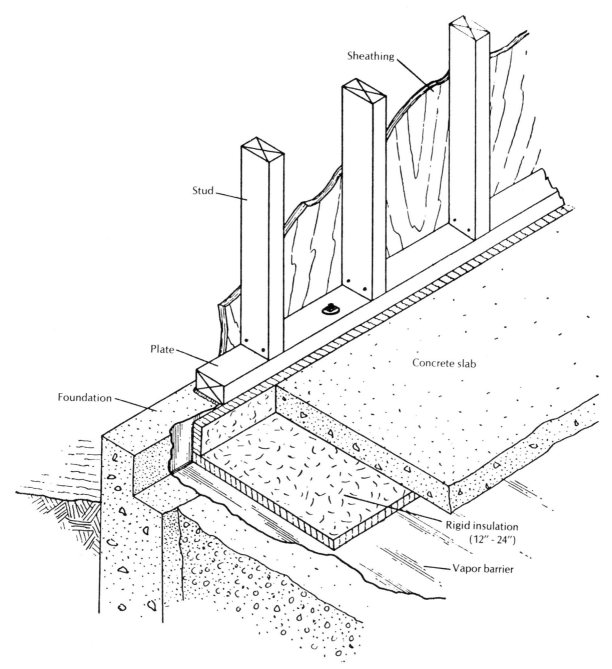

Sheathing

Stud

Plate

Foundation

Concrete slab

Rigid insulation
(12" - 24")

Vapor barrier

Fig. 6-2 Technical details of foundation, floor, and wall construction. (Courtesy USDA)

weather should turn extremely wet, you may need to cover the concrete with a tarpaulin. Too much water is not good either. You should be able to stand on the concrete within a few days, but "curing" will take about one month.

Leave an expansion joint or space between the slab and your house foundation in order to prevent buckling during hot weather. Again, check locally as to typical and correct expansion joint dimensions in your area.

The best time to pour concrete is when temperatures are about 60° F and the weather moderately dry. Pick a good day, of course. Don't be misled because you see contractors pouring con-

A section of what-was-once-the-garage could make a cozy sewing corner. (Photos by the makers of Armstrong Flooring, Carpets, and Ceiling Systems)

What an unfinished area (your garage?) can look like a few weeks from now. (Photo by the makers of Armstrong Flooring, Carpets, and Ceiling Systems)

crete in midwinter or midsummer. Their experience and formulas provide them with knowledge and skills the average do–it–yourself person isn't likely to have available (although you might stop at the site and ask questions of a friendly contractor and his crew).

Concrete–slab floors have the disadvantages of being hard and cold. Simply laying a wood floor, tile, or carpeting over the concrete won't soften and warm a concrete floor very much. Instead, lay 2 x 4's on their sides across the concrete, from wall to wall. Fasten them with concrete nails and lay plywood subflooring over the 2 x 4's ("sleepers") which should be spaced 12" apart. Wood or tile flooring or carpeting is then installed over the subfloor. This provides the "give" you need for a comfortable floor and also traps cold air coming up through the slab.

FRAMING THE WALLS

As planned, you'll be building this new room from the foundation up.

First, start with the sills (refer to Fig. 6–2). They are usually 2 x 6's covered with a wood preservative. The wood preservative is important, because without it moisture can damage the wood and the chances of fungi, wood–rotting, and termite destruction are increased. Before laying the sills, apply a sill sealer to keep out water. Instead of nailing the sills to the foundation, use anchor bolts fastened with washers and nuts.

After the carport became a den. Windows could also be sliding doors for direct exit to patio, garden. (Photo by the makers of Armstrong Flooring, Carpets, and Ceiling Systems)

The next step is to raise partitions on all three sides just as you raised partitions in the attic and basement. These outside walls, though, need to be much sturdier. In most cases 2 x 4 uprights or studs are used. However, many people now consider using 2 x 6's which can accommodate 5 1/2" insulation whereas the 2 x 4's only accommodate 3 1/2" insulation. The lumber should be of good quality: fir, hemlock, pine, or spruce; depending on local building codes.

The height of the uprights or studs is usually 7'7 1/2" because the bottom plate and the two top plates will total about 4 1/2". (Sometimes 2 x 4's are not 2" thick but 1 1/2" thick, so check the dimensions). Spacing between the studs is the traditional 16" on center, unless you use the new Mod 24 system which calls for 24" on center to save money on lumber.

To space between the studs, measure from one side of a stud to the same side of the next. This will give you spacing of 16" on center which is needed to handle 4' x 8' sheets of plywood. Or, cut a 2 x 4 exactly 14 1/2" long and use it as a spacer between the studs.

Corners are formed by nailing a 4 x 6 post at one corner on each side so that a 2 x 4 butts against it. This provides a strong corner as shown in Fig. 6–3.

You will need to make provisions for doors and windows before you complete the frame. Exterior

Hammering home subflooring. Note spacing of joists, how panel edge rests halfway across joist. (Courtesy American Plywood Association)

doors should be 36" wide x 6'8" high, and require cripples on both sides. (See page 71 for further details.) Windows will also require special spacing, headers, and cripples. (See page 109 for further details.)

After nailing the studs between the top and bottom plates, the wall is raised into position and the bottom plate nailed into the sill using 16d (3 1/2") nails. Raising the frame is a two–man job at least and great care must be taken to ensure that the wall is plumb and straight.

On the wall side of your house there are other considerations: whether to remove the siding so that the new room butts against the sheathing, or whether to let the siding stand, covering it over with a new wall. Usually, the siding is removed, making sure the new room butts flush and all exposed edges and corners are securely sealed.

Once the walls are up and the top plates secured, including that to the wall side of the house, the frame will need to be sheathed. Typical sheathing materials are plywood sheets (minimum 5/16" exterior grade), boards and fiberboard sheets. The 4' x 8' sheets of plywood can be nailed horizontally and vertically. Nails (6d) should be spaced 6" apart at the edges and 12" on the in-between studs. Allow 1/16" to 1/8" spacing between the sheets to permit expansion and contraction. See Fig. 6–4 and Fig. 6–5 for the detail.

Sheathing outside wall with plywood sheathing panels. (Courtesy American Plywood Association)

Check level of sill, shimming as necessary. (Courtesy Andersen Corporation, Bayport, Minn. 55003)

Garages can be turned into comfortable offices for those who have to or want to work at home in a quiet area. Room design by Shirley Regendahl. (Courtesy Waverly Fabrics)

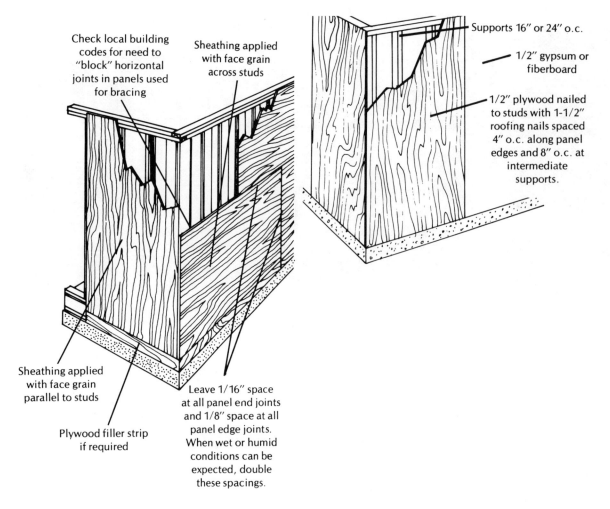

Check local building codes for need to "block" horizontal joints in panels used for bracing

Sheathing applied with face grain across studs

Supports 16" or 24" o.c.

1/2" gypsum or fiberboard

1/2" plywood nailed to studs with 1-1/2" roofing nails spaced 4" o.c. along panel edges and 8" o.c. at intermediate supports.

Sheathing applied with face grain parallel to studs

Plywood filler strip if required

Leave 1/16" space at all panel end joints and 1/8" space at all panel edge joints. When wet or humid conditions can be expected, double these spacings.

Fig. 6-3 Corner construction requires 2 x 6 posts or uprights. (Courtesy American Plywood Association)

You will also need to cover the sheathing with water–resistant sheathing paper of felt construction, overlapping the edges to ensure water repellency.

Fuel–saving insulated sheathing has become popular in the last few years. Designed to incorporate microscopic air cells into its construction, it has R values ranging from 1.14 to 2.06 adding a little extra insulation. It can be used on any nailable wall–framing and exterior–finish materials such as wood, hardboard, or aluminum siding, shingles, bricks, and stucco. It also has an advantage in that no building paper needs to be used. To fasten insulated sheathing, use 6d nails spaced 3" apart at the edges and 6" apart elsewhere.

So far, so good. The walls are up, sheathed, and sturdy.

RAISING THE ROOF

Your roof can take one of two forms. It can slant down from the side of your house just as your carport panels did, or it can be built to form a conventional peaked roof. A peaked roof has certain disadvantages in that snow can accumulate between the roof and the side of your house. On the other hand, you may feel that a roof slanting from the side of the house looks too much like the roof of a shed.

Both roof types will require ceiling joists, which can be 2 x 4's because there will be nothing above the ceiling except insulation and perhaps light storage. You will need to nail the joists from side to side, which will mean nailing a 4 x 8 or 4 x 10 along the wall side of the house. The present

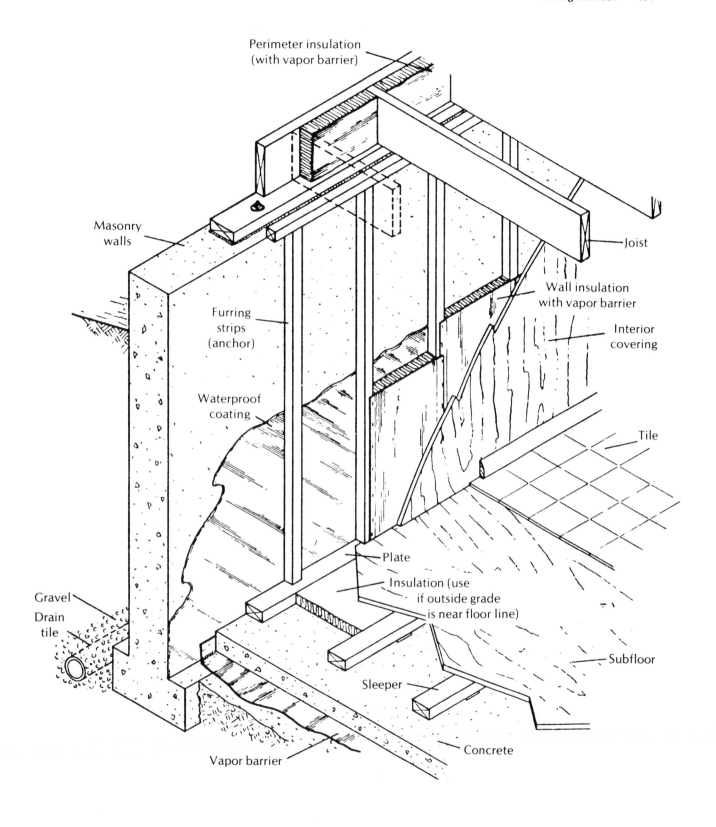

Perimeter insulation
(with vapor barrier)

Masonry
walls

Joist

Furring
strips
(anchor)

Wall insulation
with vapor barrier

Interior
covering

Waterproof
coating

Tile

Plate

Insulation (use
if outside grade
is near floor line)

Gravel

Drain
tile

Subfloor

Sleeper

Concrete

Vapor barrier

Fig. 6-4   Interior detail showing interior covering, insulation,
sheathing. (Courtesy USDA)

Plywood lap siding

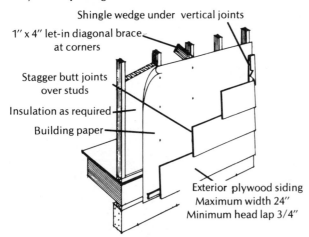

Shingle wedge under vertical joints

1″ x 4″ let-in diagonal brace at corners

Stagger butt joints over studs

Insulation as required

Building paper

Exterior plywood siding
Maximum width 24″
Minimum head lap 3/4″

Fig. 6-5 Exterior sheathing detail including insulation, sheathing, siding. (Courtesy American Plywood Association)

Plywood Gable Ends

Exterior plywood siding (may also be applied over sheathing) no building paper required with shiplap edges or battens.

Provide adequate ventilation

Fig. 6-6 Details of roof end construction showing gable ends. (Courtesy American Plywood Association)

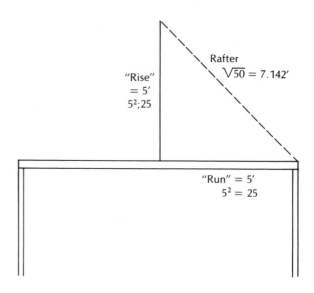

"Rise" = 5′
5^2; 25

Rafter
$\sqrt{50} = 7.142′$

"Run" = 5′
$5^2 = 25$

Fig. 6-7 How to determine the length of a rafter.

siding must be removed if the support is to be sturdy. The first joist on both ends should be set back from the top plate about 3 1/2″ to permit the installation of short studs (called "gable ends") to support the roof. See Fig. 6–5.

The pitch of the roof is most important, whether peaked or shed type. The proper pitch will help throw off snow in winter. Its angle can help absorb heat from the winter sun and resist the sun's heat during summer. Again, geographic and climate conditions must be considered.

Let's assume a 45° slope is right for this new addition to your house. You will need to figure out the length of the rafters and the angle at which they should be cut. Say the width of the room is 10′. The rise—the distance from the top plate to the ridgeboard—is 5′. The run—the horizontal distance from the outer edge of the top plate to the center of the top plate above which the ridgeboard will be located—is also 5′.

To determine the length of the rafters, you will first need to add the square of the rise to the square of the run. The answer will give you the square of the rafter length. In other words, $5^2 + 5^2$ = RL (rafter length) or 50′. The square root of 50′ is 7′ omitting the fraction (or 7.142′).

This is the distance from the top plate to the ridgeboard which is a 1 x 8 or 1 x 10 that will run the length of the room. Refer to Figure 6–7.

Actually, you'll want to make the rafters a little longer on one side to provide an overhang so that water and snow falling from the roof won't drip down beside the house. The allowance for the overhang may be 8″ or 10″ as you prefer. The rafters on the side facing the house will need to be cut shorter than 7′ to allow for the ridgeboard and butting against the house.

Trial-and-error methods are always useful. Nail a temporary stud (a 1 x 8) that is the height of the rise to the center of the top plate. Then cut a rafter to approximate length. Angle it against the top of the rise just as it would fit against the ridgeboard. Then make your trial-and-error measurements and cuts to establish the angle and length of the rafter allowing about 1/8″ or 1/4″ for expansion and contraction. Cut the remaining rafters for

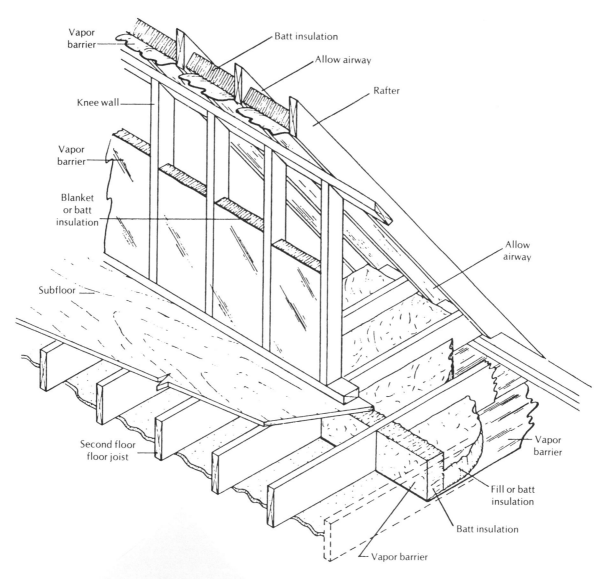

Fig. 6-8 Details of ⌐ f insulation. (Courtє

nd the run and find the square root. (For ⌐: $5^2 + 10^2 = 125$; $\sqrt{125} = 11.36'$.) Refer ⌐ig. 6-7.

⌐o cut the rafters, use an L-shaped square calibrated to indicate the angles to be cut. The angles for the run and rise show how you need to cut the rafters to fit them against the ridgeboard. Mark the angles on the first rafter.

Next you will need to notch the rafters to fit them over the top plate. Use the L-square again to

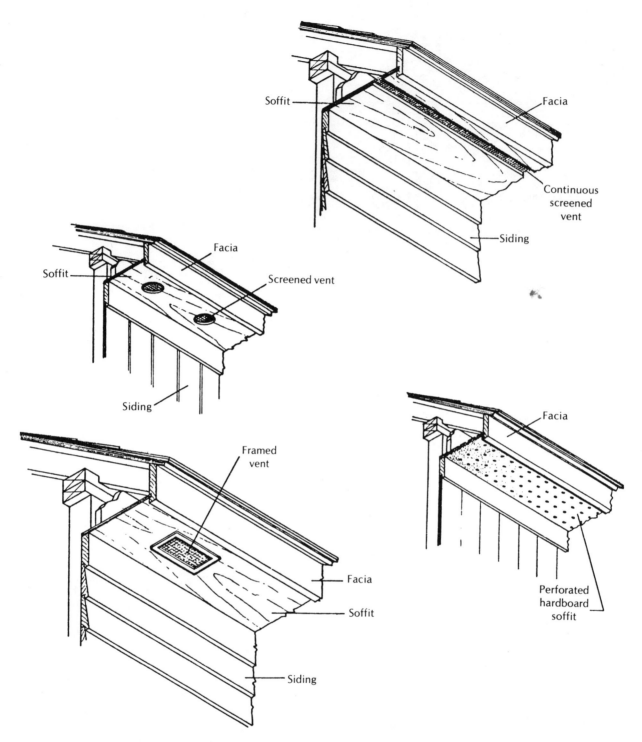

Fig. 6-9 Four methods of providing ventilation under the overhang. (Courtesy USDA)

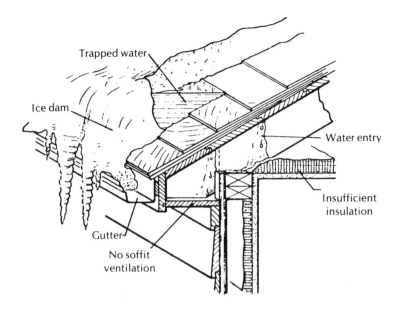

Trapped water

Ice dam

Water entry

Insufficient insulation

Gutter

No soffit ventilation

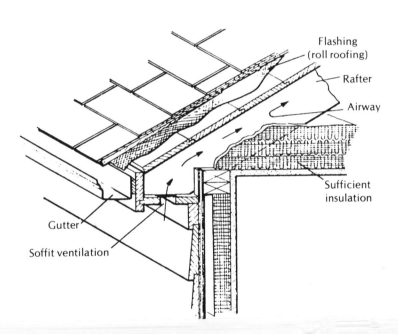

Flashing (roll roofing)

Rafter

Airway

Sufficient insulation

Gutter

Soffit ventilation

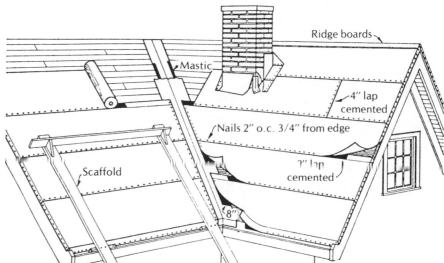

Fig. 6-11 Applying roofing paper beginning with first course or row. (Courtesy USDA)

1/16″ space at the ends and 1/8″ at the edges, more if you live in a wet, humid climate. Nail the panels down with 8d galvanized or aluminum nails spaced 6″ apart near the edges and 12″ apart elsewhere. The sheathing should continue to the edge of the overhang.

There are several ways you can finish a roof overhang. The ends of the rafters can be left as they are or cut horizontally or vertically to the ground. They can also be cut horizontally and facia, cornice and freize attached. Or, they can be cut horizontal and then fitted with lookout and facia. How you finish the overhang should depend on the overhang already on your home unless there is some reason for being drastically different. In any case, you must provide proper inlet ventilation in the soffit and sufficient insulation as shown in Fig. 6–9. Otherwise, as shown in the two drawings in Fig. 6–10, ice and water damage can result.

To do roof addition properly, you should cover the roof with roofing paper ("tarpaper"), double lapping the rolls. Unroll the paper as you work from side to side and nail with galvanized nails. See Fig. 6–11 for the detail.

Laying shingles is not a complicated job. Snap a horizontal chalkline for the first row of shingles and then a vertical chalkline (or more than one) to make sure the shingles are lined up both ways. Calculate the length of a row and the width of the shingles. A row of shingles will almost always need to be cut and it should be the first one. Overlap the shingles according to the instructions as there are several ways rows can be laid. Seal any nail

holes and any exposed nail heads with roofing cement to prevent seepage.

The peak or ridge is often the most difficult task in shingling. Cut the shingles into squares of about 1′ and fold them in half over the ridge. Overlap each shingle by at least 6″ side by side. Cover any exposed nail heads with roofing cement. Sometimes a daub of cement is added under the shingles to prevent lifting by wind or rain. See Fig. 6–12.

The area between the roof and the house will require special attention. To prevent leaks and seepage, you can't go to too far when you install flashing. You can use roofing paper, but metal flashing is much better.

Take a wide sheet of flashing, at least 9″ wide and even 12″. Fold the flashing into the corner between the house and roof but not so sharply that it cracks. Cement the shorter side to the wall and the wider side, 6″ or 8″, onto the roof. Run a seam of waterproof cement around the edges. Overlap the sections of flashing so that the lower section is always beneath the one above. Cement these seams too, but do not create ridges because you'll want water and snow to move downward evenly and freely. Do not nail shingles through the flashing. Also, allow the flashing to widen slightly as it comes down the roof, about 1/8″ per downward foot should be sufficient. If you want to shingle to the ridge of the roof you can. Allow the shingles to bend halfway up the wall while the other section remains on the roof. Again, the flashing between roof and wall is critical because

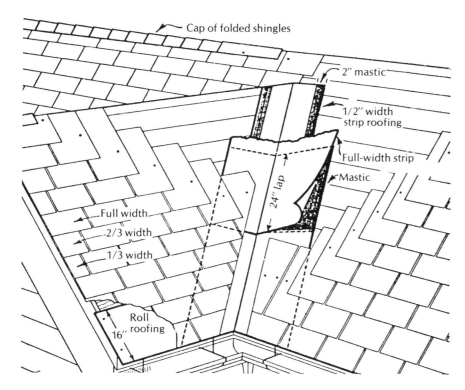

Cap of folded shingles

2″ mastic

1/2″ width strip roofing

Full-width strip

Mastic

24″ lap

Full width

2/3 width

1/3 width

Roll roofing

16″

Fig. 6-12 Shingling directions including capping ridgeboard and waterproofing valley. (Courtesy USDA)

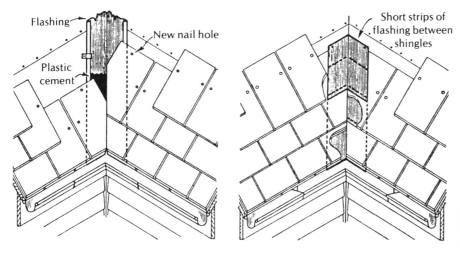

Flashing

New nail hole

Plastic cement

Short strips of flashing between shingles

Fig. 6-13 Two methods of installing flashing between the house and the addition. (Courtesy USDA)

Siding Regular Vertical Application

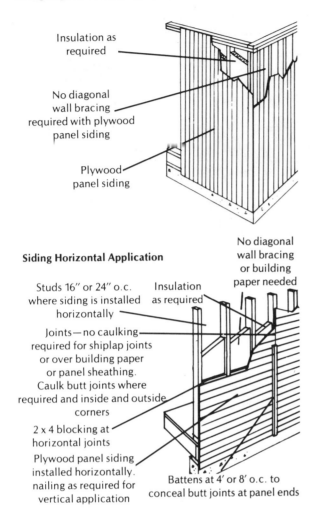

Insulation as required

No diagonal wall bracing required with plywood panel siding

Plywood panel siding

Siding Horizontal Application

No diagonal wall bracing or building paper needed

Studs 16" or 24" o.c. where siding is installed horizontally

Insulation as required

Joints—no caulking required for shiplap joints or over building paper or panel sheathing. Caulk butt joints where required and inside and outside corners

2 x 4 blocking at horizontal joints

Plywood panel siding installed horizontally. nailing as required for vertical application

Battens at 4' or 8' o.c. to conceal butt joints at panel ends

Fig. 6-14 Applying siding over plywood sheathing. (Courtesy American Plywood Association)

THE NEW ADDITION'S EXTERIOR

The easiest, most appropriate way to finish the outside of the carport or garage now enclosed as a room is to stain or paint it the same color as the rest of the house. If your house hasn't been painted for three or four years, the new paint job will stick out like a sore thumb. That means painting the entire house. Do the job, and then celebrate, because now you have a seven-room house instead of a four-room house or a nine room home instead of a six room house.

Staining is a popular exterior finish. It looks good, is easy to apply, and water resistant. Also, it doesn't require a primer. At worst, if you select a clear stain you may need to seal the knotholes. Clear and pigmented stains are available, the latter

giving you almost any color you like. You'll need to apply two coats, but once you brush or spray them on you've finished the job.

A painted house will require a painted addition. First, cover any knots in the wood (and there will be many) with shellac or a stain killer. Countersink any protruding nails and cover them with glazing. In some cases, a wood preservative may need to be applied before a primer coat. Paint the addition with primer and let it dry for several weeks before applying a finish coat or two of latex- or oil-base exterior paint.

When you purchase exterior paint, purchase at least a case at a time and check the serial numbers to make sure they all come from the same batch. Otherwise, you may get a "seam" effect from using different gallons even though they were produced by the same manufacturer and are the same color.

Paint can be applied by traditional hand brushing or spraying (rent one if the addition is large or you need to paint the entire house). Before spraying, cover the window and door edges with masking tape. Also practice using the sprayer until you get the knack of spraying evenly. Prime and paint the edges of all doors and windows to keep out moisture and to prevent the doors and windows from sticking.

SIDING THE FORMER CARPORT

Now that you have a roof over your room you'll want to finish the exterior walls with siding. Make your choice, but using the same material—clapboard, shingles, brick, stucco, aluminum, vinyl, or whatever—already used on your house makes the most sense.

Clapboard or drop siding is an old favorite. These boards, ranging in width from about 4" to 12", are slightly thicker on one side than the other, the thicker portion being the downward side. They are installed horizontally and overlapped at least one inch as shown in Fig. 6-14. Care must be taken to install the first one straight and level. Start from the foundation up, nailing the boards in the middle. Do not nail into the thin portion, for otherwise wind could get under the boards. Use nonrusting nails that can be painted over. Cutting and fitting around doors and windows will require careful measurements and accurate cuts.

Shingles are perhaps the most widely used siding, especially stained red cedar shakes. They are thinner at the "top" than the "bottom," and easily nailed to the sheathing. One advantage is that the row above covers the nails. Often the first row of shingles is doubled with a second row applied over the first, giving the house a "skirt" effect that provides the very important advantage of making water drip away from the foundation.

The first rows especially need to be level because you will be building on them all the way to the top. If a row of half-size or a smaller row of shingles is needed, the custom is to nail them at the top where they won't be seen as easily, and where they will be protected by the overhang. At corners, cut the shingles and butt them tightly together. Caulking at the corners is a good idea because the corners especially are exposed to wind and rain.

Vinyl and aluminum sidings have become very popular in recent years because they require less maintenance and may provide greater insulation and long-lasting wear. Instructions for these modern sidings come with the materials.

INSULATING THE NEW ROOM

When you have finished sheathing and siding, pay plenty of attention to insulating the new room. Remember this is an annex to the house, off the line of the main heating system, which could raise your heating costs substantially. Even though the new room should be located on the nonexposed side of the house, it is still subject to cold, wind, and sun from the other directions.

Insulating batts or rolls at least 3 1/2" thick should be used in the walls if you erected 2 x 4 uprights, or 4" to 5 1/2"-thick insulation if you used 2 x 6 uprights. Use at least the same thicknesses in the roof, stapling the insulation to the rafters but leaving 1/2" airspace between insulation and roof. Install lightweight insulating panels above the ceiling, whether you install the ceiling panels directly to the joists or suspend them. Also caulk and weatherstrip thoroughly before closing in doors and windows

Figure 6–15, and photographs 6–8 through 6–11 show the procedure for installing a sliding door. Preassembled units are available in sizes from 3'3 1/8" to 12'3" (3 panels or doors) wide, with 6'10 3/8" being a standard height.

First, lay out the opening width plus the thickness of two regular-size studs. Cut a header (usually a 2 x 12) and position it between the uprights. Next, cut jack studs (refer to illustration) and fit them under the header and nail them to the adjoining studs. Next, install the exterior sheathing flush with the header, studs, and jack studs.

Instructions for installing the sliding door or doors and windows should come with the preassembled unit. Here's what installation involves.

1. Applying compound across the opening to provide a tight, positive seal between the door sill and the floor.

2. Positioning the door frame and shimming as needed to make sure the sill is level.

3. Securing the frame to the sill by nailing 8d (2 1/2") nails approximately 12" apart.

4. Checking the door jamb for plumb and straightness, shimming as needed and nailing with 10d (3") casing nails to the side and head casing frames.

5. Securing the flashing over the door head frame.

Once the door frame is in place, the door panels are inserted and the manufacturer's instructions followed to make sure the doors slide easily and close properly.

Installing a window is a similar operation. Measure the window–opening width plus the thickness of two studs on each side. Toenail one stud to each side, checking to make sure each stud is straight and square. Cut two window headers. These are usually 2 x 6's. But you can also use 2 x 8's or 2 x 10's if you don't have 2 x 6's handy. Posi-

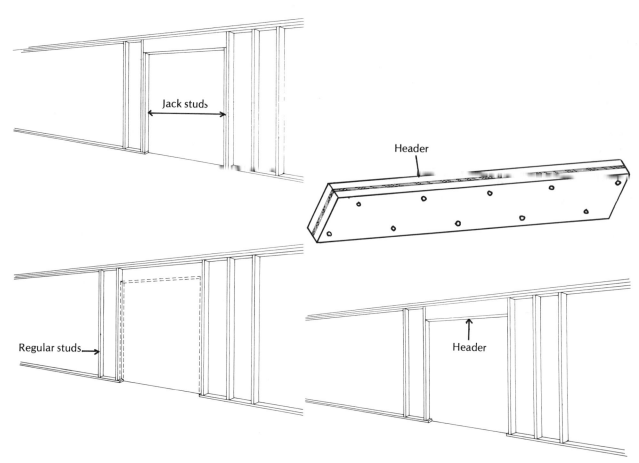

Fig. 6-15   Detail for installing a sliding door. (Courtesy Andersen Corporation, Bayport, Minn. 55003)

Nail sill to floor along inside edge using 8d coated nails. (Courtesy Andersen Corporation, Bayport, Minn. 55003)

Check jamb for plumb. Temporarily secure frame with 10d casing nails. (Courtesy Andersen Corporation, Bayport, Minn. 55003)

Position door panel by wedging door into run on side. (Courtesy Andersen Corporation, Bayport, Minn. 55003)

opening, making sure the exterior faces to the outside of the building.

First secure one corner of the window using 16d (3 1/2") casing nails. Next, check the window level across the casing and nail through the opposite casing. If necessary, place shims under the window jamb. Plumb the side jambs. Nail one lower corner and then the other before nailing through the casing on all four sides. The nails are usually spaced about 10" apart. Flashing is then applied, securing it with 1" nails. (Do *not* nail into the casing.) The window should be caulked all around after the interior siding is installed to ensure a weathertight seal.

Finish-painting a new window is essential to long-lasting, trouble-free performance. Quite often, only the window sashes are prime coated and then only on the exterior sashes. However, the rest of the unit (jambs, sill, casing) should be primed and then finish-painted. Painting around the glass edges is important to prevent water and moisture from penetrating the putty and glazing. Lap the paint approximately 1/8" onto the glass.

INSTALLING A HOUSE-TO-ADDITION DOOR

You've made pretty good progress until now. Then one of the youngsters points out you'd have to go *outside* the house to enter what used to be the carport! He's right. You completely forgot this fact while busily working on your project.

No you didn't. You left the doorway (assuming one doesn't exist) for last so you wouldn't create a mess in the house while you were working.

Here's a checklist of things to remember when you cut a doorway through an outside wall:

1. Choose a location where there is no piping; otherwise you will need to reroute that part of the system.

2. Choose a location where there is no wiring, if possible. Rewiring is not as much of a problem as reinstalling pipe. You will probably need to reroute some wiring to above the door.

3. Choose a location where there is already a window to minimize the amount of cutting needed. Also: you may be able to salvage the window and use it in the carport wall.

4. Finally, check the condition of the timbers and sheathing.

Check the location inside the house figuring on a door size of either 30" or 36" wide by 6'8" high, the usual door size. To install a 30"- or 36"- wide door with jambs you will need to cut through one or more wall studs assuming the studs are spaced 16" on center.

Check the stud locations using a studfinder. Begin cutting the wallboard or paneling inside the house. Cut carefully between the studs so that you don't inadvertently rip into wiring, piping, or crosspieces. Cut out a small section first, away from the future doorway's edges, and in the center of the area. Check inside the wall using a flashlight.

Cut out the interior wall first and then the exterior. Nail two cripples the height of the door to the studs just as you did for the sliding door (refer back to Fig. 6–15). You should not need to erect braces to support the studs above the height you plan to cut them. Unlike the sloping rafters above a roof window, the studs stand vertical and are supported by the rest of the wall. But if you have doubts, brace the studs with 2 x 4's toenailing them into the floor plate or sill.

Now cut the studs to be removed at the prescribed height and at the floor. Hammer in a 2 x 6, 2 x 8 or 2 x 10 header above the cripples. The remaining installation work is similar to that described in installing sliding doors.

STEP CONSTRUCTION

A stair or two or more may be needed to step down from the house into the new recreation room, "sports arena," or whatever the additional room may be. Steps may also be needed to the outdoors from the converted garage or carport.

Good tread and riser dimensions are 15" and 7 1/2" (including the tread) or a 2:1 ratio with the width being 30" or 36" according to the door width.

The treads and risers are supported by sloping 2 x 12's on each side, notched to support or carry the corners where the treads and risers join. If 2 x 12 seems oversize, remember that the stair carriage (the 2 x 12's) must be notched to accommodate the tread and riser. Also, the treads take the full downward thrust and weight of a person's step.

Two stair carriages may be sufficient for a one-, two- or three-step stairway. But do the job right: install a third carriage between the outer

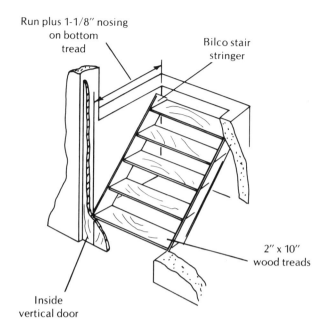

Run plus 1-1/8″ nosing
on bottom
tread

Bilco stair
stringer

2″ x 10″
wood treads

Inside
vertical door

Fig. 6-16 Step construction from house to new, added room.

two. The tread should overhang the riser by 1 1/8″ (the overhang is called the "nose") and requires full-width trim or molding to support it. For details, see Fig. 6-16.

Install the stair carriages first, notching the angles to receive the tread and risers. Then install the risers, nailing them into the carriages, and the treads last. The unit can be built in place, but it is usually easier to assemble the stairway and then place it, carefully checking and rechecking all dimensions during construction. Good solid oak is the best wood to use but is expensive. Tongue-and-groove boards were once used but almost everyone now uses single-width boards.

An outdoor concrete step or two, set down from a slab floor, is fairly easy to construct. It shouldn't require anywhere near the amount of

storm/screen door. If you have installed sliding doors, the slab or step should be as wide as the door plus 6″ more on both sides for convenience, safety, and a railing if you install one. The outward dimension should be at least 2′ for safe, sound footing.

Good concrete slabs and steps are built on footings and foundations. So excavate below the frost line, pour the footing, and then build forms constructed to form the final stairway. Next, pour the concrete, reinforcing it with rods or wire mesh. Solid fill (rocks, gravel, sand) can be used in the center of the concrete but should be thoroughly compacted.

Incidentally, it's a good idea to check with local contractors and building inspectors as to the depth of the frost line in your area because the frost line varies according to climate and altitude.

The height of the risers and the width or depth of the treads can be the same measurements used for stairs inside your house. However, the treads are frequently made wider (10″ or 12″) and the risers shorter (5″ to 7″) in order to assure the good footing essential in rainy, snowy, and icy weather. Outdoor stairs should also pitch downward 1/4″ to 1/2″ away from the house in order to provide drainage.

Bricks also make good stepping places and stairs. They are laid in concrete that has not yet hardened (the same day the concrete is poured), and then mortared on the surfaces and between the sides. Different patterns, such as herringbone, can be laid with brick for a pleasing effect. Wood stairs can also be constructed provided they have a solid foundation.

This small book couldn't tell you everything you'd like to know about renovating your unfinished attic, basement, carport, or garage. But it should help guide you through your project, and

ACKNOWLEDGMENTS

The author wishes to thank the following organizations for their assistance in furnishing literature and illustrations for this book:

American Olean Tile Company, Lansdale, Penna. 19446

American Optical Corporation, Safety Products Division, Southbridge, Mass. 01550

American Plywood Association, Tacoma, Wash. 98401

Andersen Corporation, Bayport, Minn. 55003

Armstrong Cork Company, Lancaster, Penna. 17604

The Bilco Company, New Haven, Conn. 06505

Bird & Son, Inc., East Walpole, Mass. 02032

E.L. Bruce Co., Inc., Memphis, Tenn. 38116

Burlington Industries, Inc., Carpet Division, King of Prussia, Penn. 19406

CertainTeed Corporation, Valley Forge, Penna. 19482

Champion International Corporation, Champion Building Products, Stamford, Conn. 06921

Collins & Aikman Inc. New York, New York 10016

Evans Products Company, Grossman's Division, Braintree. Mass. 02164

Flintkote Company, Building Materials Division, East Rutherford, New Jersey 07073

Georgia–Pacific Corporation, Portland, Ore. 97204

W.R. Grace & Co., Construction Products Division, Cambridge, Mass. 02140

National Gypsum Company, Gold Bond Building Products, Buffalo, New York 14202

Paeco, Inc., Perth Amboy, New Jersey 08861

PLAN–IT–KIT, Inc., Westport, Conn. 06880

Plywood Ranch Industries, Inc., Woburn, Mass. 01801

The Savogran Company, Norwood, Mass. 02062

Tile Council of America, Inc., Princeton, New Jersey 08540

U.S. Department of Agriculture, Washington, D.C. 20402

United States Gypsum Company, Chicago, Ill. 60606

Velux–America, Inc., Woburn, Mass. 01801

Waverly Fabrics, a division of F. Schumacher &

BIBLIOGRAPHY

American Insurance Association, Engineering and Safety Service. *The National Building Code*, New York, 1976.

Branden, F. Van Den; and Hartsell, Thomas L. *Plastering Skill and Practice*. 2nd ed., Chicago: American Technical Society, 1974.

Brann, Donald R. *Electrical Repairs Simplified*. Rev. ed., Briarcliff Manor, New York: Directions Simplified, Inc. 1975.

Brann, Donald R. *How to Modernize an Attic*. Rev. ed., Briarcliff Manor, New York: Directions Simplified, Inc., 1974.

Brann, Donald R. *Plumbing Repairs Simplified*. Rev. ed., Briarcliff Manor, New York: Directions Simplified, Inc., 1976.

Bright, James L. *The Home Repair Book*. Chicago: J.G. Ferguson Publishing Company, 1977.

Daniels, George. *Home Guide to Plumbing, Heating and Air Conditioning*. New York: Popular Science Publishing Co., Harper & Row, 1972.

Day, Richard. *The Practical Handbook of Electrical Repairs*. New York: Arco Publishing Com-

Ewers, William. *Solar Energy, A Biased Guide*. Northbrook, Illinois: Domus Books, 1977.

Gladstone, Bernard. *The N.Y. Times Complete Manual of Home Repair*. New York: The Macmillan Company, 1965.

Hotton, Peter. *So You Want to Build a House*. Boston: Little, Brown and Company, 1976.

Matthias, A. J.; Smith, Esles; Volland, Robert J. *How to Design and Install Plumbing*. 4th Ed. Chicago: American Technical Society, 1975.

3M Company (Minnesota Mining & Manufacturing). *The Home Pro Electrical Installation and Repair Guide*. 1975.

3M Company (Minnesota Mining & Manufacturing). *The Home Pro Plumbing Guide*. 1975.

Oravetz, Jules, Sr. *Plumbers' and Pipe Fitters' Library*. Indianapolis: Howard W. Sams & Co., Inc., 1973.

Schuler, Stanley. *All Your Home Building and Remodeling Questions Answered*. New York: The Macmillan Company, 1971.

GLOSSARY

Blocking crosspieces used between uprights (or "studs") to support paneling or drywall construction.

Casing the framework around a door or window.

Carriage *see* Stringer

Cat sometimes used as another name for a crosspiece

Chalkline a chalk–rubbed piece of string stretched taut between two points on a surface, then plucked or snapped to mark a straight line.

Circuit the closed path followed by electrical current from the control panel (or point of entry), through the home, and back to the control panel.

Cold chisel A chisel made to cut cold metal.

Corner beads narrow strips of molding used to define or protect interior wall corners.

Cornice horizontal molding or projection at the meeting of a roof and an exterior wall.

Cripple a shorter length of wood used beside a door or window.

Crosspiece a horizontal piece of lumber used between upright (or studs) to support paneling or other drywall construction

Crosstee part of the support grid (with runners) for a suspended ceiling.

Drywall wall materials such as wallboard, gypsumboard, sheetrock, fiberboard, hardboard, plywood—which do not require mixing materials such as plaster with water.

Facia a horizontal board between the top of an exterior wall and the projecting eaves.

Feather to spread an adhesive or compound so that it spreads out lightly (as a bird's feather).

Fishing locating and pulling electrical cable to one opening from another in the wall, or through a floor and ceiling.

Float a tool used to smooth a newly poured concrete surface.

Flashing sheet metal used as weatherproofing in roof and wall construction.

Floor plate [**shoe**] a piece of lumber that runs horizontally at the bottom edge of a framed wall.

Flux a substance that promotes the fusing of metals to be soldered together.

Frieze a horizontal band of wood located below the cornice at the top of an exterior wall.

Furring strips thin strips of wood, usually 1" to 2" wide, ¼–½" thick and 4' long, used as backing for plaster and sometimes paneling

Grout[ing] a plaster or cement applied between tiles and also to the back or unseen side of tiles.

Header   a wooden beam that is fitted at right angles to and supports the free ends of joists or rafters.

Jack post   a telescoping steel post used to jack up sagging floors.

Jamb   an upright or stud used as the side of an opening such as a door.

Joists   parallel beams that support floors or ceilings.

K factor   a measure of the quantity of heat that passes through given materials in one hour.

Kneewall   a very short wall between the floor and a sloping ceiling or roof.

Lookout   a piece of lumber that runs between the ends of the rafters and the outside wall.

Miter   to cut or bevel two pieces of wood at angles so they form a miter joint, both pieces being flush with each other.

Mortise   a hole cut in a piece of wood into which will fit a similarly shaped piece (tenon).

Nose   the part of a stair tread that projects forward over the riser below.

Pitch   a slope or angle but also a tarry substance used to seal around chimneys, flashing, pipes.

Plumbline   a weighted piece of string hung to determine a straight vertical line.

Rise   the vertical distance between the tops of the walls and the highest point of the roof (the ridge).

Risers   the vertical components of a stairway, also vertical pipes in a plumbing system.

Roll roofing   asphalt–impregnated felt.

Roof deck   sheathing that is nailed over rafters, and to which roofing materials will be attached.

Run   the distance between an exterior wall and the center of the area to be roofed over.

Scribing   using a compass to outline indented, irregular, or circular short distances around windows, doors, etc. so that the tile or wallpaper will fit flush.

Sealant   a sealing agent.

Shim [shimming]   a small wedge or sliver of wood put between frame openings and windows or doors to ensure level installations. Shims are used to adjust spaces and positions in many types of installations.

Shoe [floor plate]   a 2 x 4″ piece of lumber placed across the floor in order to form a support for the studs of a partition.

Sleepers   lengths of wood or other material that lie on the foundation or embedded in concrete and support the floor joists.

Solder   a metal alloy that is melted and used to join metal surfaces.

Stapling flange   the edges of a piece of ceiling tile that are meant to be stapled to the furring strips or other anchor.

Strike plate   hardware installed in a door jamb to receive the latch bolt.

Stringer [carriage]   the piece of wood that is cut out to receive the treads and risers; the stair support.

Stud   an upright piece of lumber used to support the top plate of a partition in order to form a wall.

Subflooring [underlayment]   flooring that lies underneath the finished surface.

Toenailing   nailing diagonally through a vertical upright or stud into a horizontal piece of lumber (usually a floor plate or shoe).

Top plate   a horizontal piece of lumber that tops a framed wall.

Tread   the horizontal component of a stairway.

U factor   the hourly rate of heat fl

INDEX